Miss Elvira Ivey

Dr. Fay Stapleton Burnett

Front Cover: Double-Barrel Shotgun, courtesy Franklin's Gun Shop, Athens, Ga.; Wooden cut-out of Georgia, purchased at Mulberry and Magnolia Gift Shop, Louisville, Ga., made by Adam Brett from reclaimed heart-pine of old house in Jefferson County, Ga.

My sincere thanks to all those who shared photographs, helped me look up books, gave me information and acted as "gate-keepers" to allow me to make vital contacts. It would be impossible to have a successful project without folks willing to give a helping hand.

Copyright: © 2019 Dr. Fay Stapleton Burnett; all rights reserved.

Printed: Kindle Direct Publishing

ISBN: 9781791623623

Dedication

I would like to dedicate this book to all those who have encouraged me along my life's journey – both alive and those gone on to Glory. It is with a great sense of gratitude that I also offer thanks to my Lord and Savior Jesus Christ, who guides and directs my paths…and will ultimately greet me in Heaven when this life's journey is ended.

Contents

Page

Introduction..7

Her Story..11

Just My Opinion...35

Lessons Learned...43

The Rest of the Story..................................47

Appendix:

    Exhibit (1) Thomas E. Watson & W. D. Tutt.................55
    Exhibit (2) Birth Date of Elvira Ivey.............................66
    Exhibit (3) Disparity – Males and Females....................66
    Exhibit (4) Lore from the Extended Ivey Family............67
    Exhibit (5) The Description of Elvira Ivey in the Press....68
    Exhibit (6) List of Lawyers for Elvira's Court Cases........69
    Exhibit (7) News Sources – Elvira Ivey.........................69
    Exhibit (8) News Sources – Murder of Solomon Jones...105

Gallery..113

Introduction

It seems unlikely that someone who has such distaste for the subject of murder would be found in this position. For the second time in the span of two years, I was compelled to research and write a book about a Georgia female in the late 1800s charged with murder.

Both cases were discovered as the result of research for a book relating to the 1885-1888 journal of my Great-Grandfather, Col. Rev. James Stapleton of Jefferson County, Georgia. Upon putting the word-search in a data base of historic newspapers online, I discovered the first story, which concerned the hanging of Susan Eberhart in 1873. My connection to this case was through my Great-Great-Grandfather, Maj. Rev. George Lawson Stapleton, Jr., who said the final prayer on the gallows with Susan Eberhart before she was hanged for murder in Preston, Georgia. That discovery took me on an incredible journey, which led to the publication of my first book, "The Hanging of Susan Eberhart."

After setting aside my initial project for over a year, I picked up the journal and began in earnest to transcribe…only to be sidetracked again. There were three murders mentioned in the journal, one of which was the trial of Miss Elvira Ivey for the murder of Jack McCauley. James Stapleton documents this topic several times in his journal as follows:

Feb. 17, 1885, Tuesday: …Large numbers of persons gone to Louisville to day to attend the commitment trial of Miss Vira Ivey for the killing of Mr. Jack McCawley.

May 11, 1885, Monday: ...I and J. D. Stapleton went to Louisville this Court week. J. D. was on the jury but the judge excused him. – There was a large crowd present – several criminal cases to try...

May 12, 1885, Tuesday: James gone to Louisville to attend Court – he was summoned as a juror. [Reference to Col. James' son, James Stapleton Jr.]

May 14, 1885, Thursday: ...Large numbers attending Court, as witnesses and spectators in the Miss Vira Ivey case for the murder of Jack McCawley.

My Great-Grandfather showed restraint in his minimal mention of the murder and a total lack of the associated gossip – as undoubtedly, there were many tongues wagging.

It was a sensational murder for any location, but especially in the rural county of Jefferson in East-central Georgia. It brings to mind the saying, *"There's not much to see in a small town, but what you hear makes up for it."* The story was covered in almost all the newspapers in the state of Georgia, as well as many throughout the nation, including The *New York Times* and *Courrier des Etats-Unis,* (a French newspaper published in New York, founded by the older brother of Napoleon Bonaparte.)

The case of Miss Elvira Ivey occurred eleven years after the case of Susan Eberhart. Gov. James Milton Smith, who refused to commute the sentence of Susan Eberhart, was never forgiven for his failure to show mercy – and therefore was never elected to office again. Every succeeding governor knew their fate would be the same; in Georgia, if you let a white woman "swing" from the gallows, your career was over. The residents of Georgia were very familiar with Susan Eberhart, as her story was widely covered in the press and a great topic of conversation. The case continued to be mentioned for decades whenever a white woman in Georgia was charged with murder. I believe the consequences experienced by Governor Smith relative to Susan Eberhart played a pivotal role in the actions of Elvira Ivey when she found herself in the unenviable position of a murdered lover at her window.

There was a great deal of mystery surrounding the murder of Jack McCauley, and though Elvira confessed to the crime, it was widely speculated that she did not pull the trigger. The truth in the case of Miss Elvira Ivey will never be known with any certainty; but one thing is certain – *she was a most beautiful woman.*

Her Story

Miss Sansil Elvira Ivey was born on December 20th, 1863 in Warren County, Georgia - a rural area, about 60 miles west of Augusta, Georgia. Warren County in the 1800s was an agricultural community, with lots of cotton plantations, which meant lots of slaves.

December is such a lovely month to give birth, with all the festivities and good cheer of Christmas; but as it happened, Elvira was born in the middle of the Civil War. In 1863, the South still had hopes of winning the war, but by the time Elvira was almost one year old, Gen. William Tecumseh Sherman's troops were knocking on the door of Warren County…or more accurately, barging in with lots of matches. For those of us raised in Georgia whose ancestors lived through this period, it is not necessary to say the full name…only "Sherman" needs to be heard, and a chill runs down our spines. As the Union troops passed through this area of Georgia, a path of burning and destruction was left on their five-week "March to the Sea" as they headed from Atlanta to the Georgia coast. Along with burning structures, horses and other animals were killed; train tracks were destroyed; pillaging and theft occurred; men were "insulted," and women were "assaulted." Southerners no doubt exaggerate some of the details of this campaign, while Northerners no doubt minimize some details, *so*, the truth probably lies somewhere in between the two versions. Not wishing to reignite another conflict, let's just agree; it was bad.

The day after Elvira's first birthday, Dec. 21, 1864, Gen. Sherman reached the Atlantic Ocean and presented the city of Savannah as a Christmas gift to President Lincoln the next day. The Civil War continued on until April of 1865, when Gen. Robert E. Lee surrendered the Army of Northern Virginia to Gen. Ulysses S. Grant at Appomattox, Virginia. Life continued to be difficult in the South after the end of the war. "Reconstruction" was painful and slow, following the "demolition" of the Civil War. After the emancipation of the slaves at the end of the War, racial tensions were running high. Gold had been converted to Confederate paper currency during the war – which had become worthless. Homes, farms and barns were burned or destroyed. This time of hardship and turmoil was the environment of Elvira's childhood.

A high number of men were killed or disabled during the Civil War, making it difficult for women to wed. The disparity between men and women was especially significant in the South, and the social impact of this fact cannot be overstated. Competition for men was stiff, and no doubt some women resorted to whatever means possible to attract and keep a man. Women who were not fortunate enough to wed became "old maids," dependent on others for their upkeep unless they inherited their own fortune or somehow found employment.

The Ivey family had 11 children, which was not unusual in that era. Adam Ivey, Elvira's father, was a farmer and owned his own farmland. The Ivey family was somewhat average or upper middle income. It should be noted that families of this income level who were farmers in Warren and surrounding counties did *not* live the kind of lives depicted for the O'Hara family in "Gone With the Wind." Though they had assets, their lifestyle was much more modest. Not much is published about the Ivey family during the period of reconstruction, but presumably their life was similar to others in Warren County at that time - very difficult. By the year 1884, when the murder occurred, life was improving in the South. The economy was better, money was circulating in the system, food was more available, and by comparison "happy days" were returning.

The one facet of the Ivey family that was not "average," was the appearance of their seventh child – a daughter named Sansil Elvira. She was *beautiful*. This will be mentioned many times throughout this book and cannot be stressed enough. *That single fact* most likely led to the most significant events in Elvira's life – not only the "moral failing" of Elvira, but her involvement with murder and ultimate acquittal. Apparently Elvira's looks went well beyond being pretty. She was exceptionally beautiful, and almost every single newspaper article made note of this fact.

In the case of Susan Eberhart, (the young white woman hanged in 1873), she came from a dirt poor family, and was noted as being "not unattractive, but not beautiful." When Susan Eberhart was discussed, she was almost always referred to as simply "Susan Eberhart;" only rarely was she called "Miss Susan Eberhart." Quite the opposite was true of Elvira. She was almost always referred to as "Miss Elvira Ivey." Both women were about the same age when the murders occurred; Elvira did come from a family with more money and class than the Eberharts, but her striking beauty was inescapable. Women of exceptional beauty, whether it be in Biblical times, or 1885, or 2019, always garner more courtesy and favors than unfortunate females who are simply "plain." Elvira was even referred to as a "murderess," a term *not* often used to describe Susan Eberhart. It's almost as if the term "murderess" conveyed a certain degree of respect.

The beginning of Elvira's troubles can be traced back to Solomon Jones, or so she said. Elvira stated in 1885; "*My troubles commenced about six or seven years ago. I was seduced by Sol. Jones.*" This meant her "troubles" began when she was about 15 years old in the year 1878. Once Elvira's troubles began, they not only continued, but escalated. One could say Elvira Ivey was a girl with a "reputation," *not* in a good sense of the word. Elvira was engaged to Sol. Jones at one time, and he supposedly "ruined" her – which was a polite way of saying he had sexual relations with her and that she was no longer a virgin. (This also could have been a way of referring to a pregnancy out of wedlock.) Elvira's father initially insisted that Jones marry his daughter, but Jones refused. This led Mr. Ivey to bring charges against Jones for "seduction." If the community was not already aware of Elvira's reputation *before* the court case, they certainly became aware afterwards when the suit was filed in the Superior Court of Warren County. Solomon Jones married his wife Mary Seay in 1882, which was around the time he was charged with the criminal offense of seduction.

The lawyers in the seduction case were some of the most noted of the day. The attorney for Solomon Jones was Thomas E. Watson of McDuffie County, and the lead attorney for Elvira Ivey was Col. W. D. Tutt, of Augusta, formerly of McDuffie County. To have these two attorneys involved in a legal case on opposing sides made for high drama in the courtroom. The same two attorneys would find themselves in opposing corners in Elvira's manslaughter case. It is fair to say that there had been "bad blood" between Watson and Tutt for many years, tracing back to the day in 1876 when Watson arrived back home in Thomson to begin his legal practice. Tutt was the established "old dog" in the legal community, and did not take too kindly to the young upstart, Watson. Their bitter rivalry eventually culminated in Watson actually shooting Tutt in the hand in 1882, while at a law office in Thomson. Watson was charged with "attempted murder," but interestingly was later cleared in court. (The appendix of this book contains more information concerning the lives and rivalry of Watson and Tutt.)

It was often the case at that time for a person to be charged with "breach of promise" when a marital engagement was broken. This would have been a civil matter, not necessarily involving a sexual relationship. This was *not* the case for Elvira Ivey. The seduction case against Sol. Jones was *not* just a civil matter; it was of a criminal nature.

It would appear that in the midst of the Sol Jones seduction legal proceedings, Elvira began an intimate relationship with a married man in the community, Jack McCauley – the man who was later murdered. In a letter to the editor of the Augusta Chronicle, Tom Watson stated that, "*McCauley had repeatedly expressed his entire sympathy with the prosecution of Jones, and had expressed his willingness to aid that prosecution, if necessary, with his money.*" It was said that Sol. Jones and Jack McCauley had not been on speaking terms for three years leading up to the murder of McCauley –as they were rivals for the affections of Elvira. This rivalry was said to be "well known." It was hinted at in the press that Sol. Jones continued a romantic relationship with Elvira during the time they were adversaries in court, when he was married to someone else. It was also said that many attempts to settle the case brought by Mr. Ivey against Sol. Jones for seduction had been made, but with no success. This case was still pending at the time of Jack McCauley's murder.

McCauley, who lived near the Little Briar Creek Church in Warren County, was one of the wealthiest farmers in the area, and had a wife and two children. Mr. and Mrs. McCauley had not lived happily together for several years, and Jack McCauley's "criminal intimacy" with Elvira caused "many eruptions in the home…"[1] No doubt Jack McCauley had feelings of guilt from his infidelity, and would (repeatedly) try to reconcile with his wife.

About two weeks before the murder, McCauley's wife finally separated from him. It was described as a "storm [that] bursted forth with increased fury." One

---

[1] The *Warrenton Clipper*, 14 Dec., 1884.

could guess she had finally just had enough of his infidelity. Plus, there was the little issue of Elvira's pregnancy.

Several months before the murder, Elvira moved from her father's home in Warren County to her brother's house (John Marion Ivey) in Jefferson County, located not far from the Reedy Creek Baptist Church. Elvira said she moved there because of threats and harassment from Jones and his friends over the seduction case; however, she also probably moved to finish out her pregnancy and give birth away from the gossiping neighbors in Warren County. Elvira claimed that threats against her life were made by Jones and his emissaries. She also recounted that lewd and obscene *pictures* and *writings* were posted on her father's door, churches, trees, fences and other places.

It seems unimaginable that lewd or nude pictures *of* Elvira existed; however, tobacco companies at that time were putting pictures of "naked maidens" on their packages. So perhaps someone used these as part of the "placards" to humiliate and threaten Elvira. There were also nudes used in ads for saloons and tonics at that time, so these may also have been part of the "artwork" as well. These placards must have created quite a sensation for churches, and most likely involved Little Briar Creek Baptist Church and Reedy Creek Baptist Church. (James Stapleton was the circuit pastor of Little Briar Creek during the time of these events, and was a member of Reedy Creek, the home church of the Stapleton family since 1817. There was no mention of these events in James Stapleton's journal, as the diary began *after* the time of the obscene pictures and writings, but James certainly would have known about these attempts to humiliate Elvira.) Elvira reported that this kind of harassment continued when she moved to her brother's house – so, trouble followed her. Nowhere was it suggested the identity of the person responsible for placing the lewd and obscene pictures and writings, but the implication was that either Sol. Jones or some of his acquaintances or relatives were involved.

Letters were exchanged between Elvira and Jack McCauley during their two year affair, and the letters during the last year were saved by McCauley. These letters were not sent in the mail, but by a "courier." A black man named Guss Hobbs would take the letters passed between the two lovers, which were not addressed or signed, with a single exception; one letter bearing the signature of "S. E. Ivey"– which was signed *twice*, with different inks. This specific letter was the last one received by McCauley before his murder. Mrs. McCauley would later recount that she had seen the letter, though it was received *after* she left her husband. The letters were locked in a table drawer, (the key to which hung on a nearby mantle), and these letters would prove to be of great consequence and detrimental to Elvira in her first trial.

Jack McCauley met Guss Hobbs in Warrenton on Friday, Dec. 5, 1884, and asked Guss to deliver a letter to Elvira at her brother's house in Jefferson County. Guss complied, and brought a return letter to McCauley, which was admitted into evidence at the trial, this being the letter with Elvira's "duplicate signatures," and read as follows:

"Mr._____: *I have nothing to write that would interest you. I have not time to write much to you. I will go with you if you will come Friday after the first Sunday. Come below the house in that pine thicket, and I will see you after dark. Come to the window and I will give you my clothes. I will look for you. I think you have told falsehoods enough on me to send your soul to hell. I am sorry you and your wife have parted. If you can't live with her I am afraid you won't live* with me. When we leave we will never come back here no more. Get you a home before you come after me. Good-bye. Be sure to come; be particular."[2]

Sometime in the days preceding his murder, Jack made the trip to Augusta and withdrew $2,000 from a bank account, which was quite a large sum of money – the modern equivalent would be about $50,000.

One week after receiving these instructions from Elvira, Friday night, Dec. 12, 1884, would be Jack McCauley's last night alive. Based on one account, earlier that afternoon, McCauley had visited with Elvira in Jefferson County. The moon was waning that Friday night and was about 20% full, which provided some moonlight for travel, but of course not as much as a full moon. (Travel on horseback with no moonlight would have been almost impossible.) It is estimated that McCauley traveled about 6 miles or so from his farm to Elvira's brother's home, which may have taken about an hour. He rode on a single horse – not by buggy, and not taking another horse for Elvira. This fact would be mentioned in later speculation about the case.

Here is where the story becomes a jumbled mess of information, or misinformation. Elvira claimed that a between 2 and 3 o'clock on the morning of December 13th, she heard someone knocking on the window of a room adjoining her bedroom. She supposedly went to investigate, at which time she claimed that someone jerked open the window and said, *"Come and go with me and I will give you fifteen hundred dollars."* Being very afraid and not knowing who it was (so she claimed) she pulled away from the window, at which time the person said, *"If you don't hand out your things and come with me, I will blow your brains out."* She supposedly handed out a box of clothes and a pair of shoes, pretending to

---

[2] The *Savannah Morning News*, 21 May, 1885.

comply, and then went and got a gun from across the room, laid the shotgun on the window sill and fired. There were varying reports as to the weapon used. Some said it was a pistol, others said it was a rifle or a gun that belonged to McCauley himself. The most reliable information seems to be that the gun was a double-barrel shotgun, belonging to Elvira's brother John.

After the shooting, Elvira *said* she went and told her brother and father what had occurred, OR they heard the shot and came to investigate, OR?

The next morning, neighbors were summoned to the bloody scene of Jack McCauley's murder. One neighbor noted that he arrived about 10 a.m. Abel Russell was the only neighbor named in press reports. Several observations were made when the crime scene was inspected; McCauley had $1,500 (in some reports $1,590) in cash in his pocket, OR on the ground under his person, OR clutched in his left hand…depending on which report one read. ($410 was missing from the original amount of $2,000 when his body was inspected.) It was also noted that he had an open pocket knife in his right-hand britches pocket. There was a pair of lady's shoes and a paper box with some clothing nearby on the ground. As for the fatal gunshot: one report said that "the load entered one side of his mouth, and ranged down through his neck and shoulder." Another report stated that a "bullet had pierced his temple." It was described by yet another as "the load entering the left cheek and penetrating the base of the brain." No doubt a double-barrel shotgun at close range would produce a devastating effect.

A coroner's inquest was held on the Monday following the murder on Friday night and news of the inquest was reported in the *Savannah Morning News* the following day. Elvira Ivey confessed at the inquest that she shot Jack McCauley, but there was doubt about her story from the beginning. Many folks immediately speculated that Elvira was covering for another unnamed person, possibly her father or her brother.

At some point soon after the coroner's inquest, Elvira Ivey "mysteriously disappeared," which no doubt fueled the gossip mills even more. Friends of Jack McCauley conducted a search for Elvira, but with no success.

One news source stated that a preliminary trial was to be held on January 1st at Pope Hill (Wrens). Apparently Elvira was still in hiding and did not attend this trial. Throughout the discussion of this case, the terms "preliminary trial, commitment trial and preliminary hearing" will be used to describe the same legal proceeding. Whatever it may have been called, it was a hearing to determine whether probable cause existed to try a person for the crime charged, based on the evidence. It was not a private hearing, as in a Grand Jury.

Elvira's uncle, Tom Ivey, (who was reportedly an ex-convict) knew her whereabouts and was attempting to make arrangements for two weeks for Elvira to give herself up to authorities in secret, so as to avoid the spectacle of a commitment trial, or so he said. The Sheriff of Jefferson County, George Kelley, got wind of Tom Ivey's plans and posted a lookout on the road and arrested Elvira on Feb. 9th before she could reach the courthouse in Louisville. Sheriff Speir of McDuffie County also arrested Elvira's Uncle Tom at the same time, as he had warrants against him for "forgery, perjury and carrying concealed weapons, swindling, cheating, etc." Tom Ivey proclaimed his innocence, and said he could prove himself not guilty of the charges. One source put the location of the arrest as Pope Hill.

Tuesday, February 17th 1885 was an exciting day in Louisville, Georgia. Many people flocked to the commitment trial of Elvira Ivey. Not only was this a sensational crime shrouded with mystery, but no doubt some just wanted to get a look at the "beautiful Elvira Ivey." The Jefferson County courthouse was full of people "from far and near," both black and white. It was reported that the commitment trial was conducted by J. W. White, notary public. Among the witnesses was Abel Russell, who recounted Elvira's testimony from the coroner's inquest, as well as his observations from the crime scene. Mr. W. S. Thompson also presented testimony that he observed Jack McCauley's widow remove letters that were locked up in the house of the deceased. The attorney for the state in this commitment trial was Hon. F. H. Colley of Washington, and Messrs, Tutt and Gamble presented an "able and eloquent defense" in behalf of Elvira. Other members of her defense team were Phillips and Wren of Louisville, and Lockhart of Augusta. It was said in the press, *"The case is a very strong one; the lawyers, and indeed others, declaring that they had never read or heard tell of another similar one."*[3] Another source was quoted, *"The case is an interesting and mysterious one and will be a celebrated one in the court annals of the State."*[4]

Initially Elvira claimed that she did not know the identity of the man at the window when she shot. Later she said that she thought it was McCauley but was not certain. She went on to claim that she was only "casually acquainted with McCauley and had never written to him and was only in his company a few times." Oddly, Elvira also claimed that when McCauley tried to make her leave with him, she pointed out *to him* his duty to his wife and children. (McCauley and his wife had a nine year-old son and a six year-old daughter, and had been married about twelve years.) Elvira went so far as to suggest that Sol. Jones,

---

[3] The *Weekly Constitution* (Atlanta), 24 Feb., 1885.
[4] The *True Citizen* (Waynesboro, Ga.), 27 Feb., 1885.

with the help of his uncle James Norris, *hired* Jack McCauley to seduce, kidnap or murder her.

Various news sources said that the trial of Sol. Jones for seduction was to take place on the Monday following the murder of McCauley – suggesting this as a reason Jones wanted to "get Elvira out of the way." Tom Watson refuted this, stating that the only sessions of Superior Court in Warren County were held in April and October, and therefore the suggestion that the case would be in court on Monday December 15th was absolutely false. Elvira persisted in this "version" of the event, which she used to explain her actions as "self-defense."

Elvira Ivey was charged with voluntary manslaughter at her commitment trial, and bond for release was set at $1,500. Her trial was set for the May 1885 session of Jefferson County Superior Court. It was noted at this later trial that her "*cheeks showed the bleaching of her long confinement in jail*,"[5] so it appears that she was *not* released on bond after her initial incarceration until the time of the trial in May. There was no mention as to why she was not released, but perhaps her family did not have the cash to make her bond. One can speculate that the protracted legal battle involving Sol Jones for seduction may have drained the family's assets. There was a later mention of her incarceration in The *Sun* (New York) stating that "*Miss Ivey was arrested and placed under the surveillance of the Sheriff for two months. Such was the sympathy of the people for the unfortunate woman that the Sheriff allowed her all the liberty of the jail consistent with security.*"

A member of the extended Ivey family shared the following concerning Elvira's time while incarcerated: "*The Warden* [Sheriff] *took Elvira for buggy rides on*

---

[5] The *Macon Weekly Telegraph* (Macon, Ga.), 22 May, 1885.

Sundays. He also provided her with a sewing machine, as she was a good seamstress. Elvira was given material to make sheets, pillowcases and towels for the inmates in jail, and was also given material to make her own clothes." As the press reported that Elvira was in jail for two months, and there was a period of three months between her commitment trial and her criminal trial, was there perhaps a period of a month that she was *not* in jail? This raises the question as to when Elvira gave birth. The pregnancy was mentioned in one of the letters (undated) written by Elvira to McCauley, and by May of 1885 when Elvira went to trial for murder, she appeared with an "infant" on her lap. This would indicate that the baby was less than a year in age, possibly born sometime between May of 1884 and May of 1885. There is no record of the baby's birth, so it is also possible the baby was born before the murder, *or* after the murder but before her arrest. It is of course possible that Elvira may have given birth while in jail. While there was no mention of this event in the press, family members have heard this rumored and it was part of the family "lore." It is not known who fathered the child, but presumably it was McCauley's.

An estimated crowd of 500 people showed up for the sensational criminal trial of Elvira Ivey on Thursday, May 17th, 1885 in Louisville. It had all the elements needed for high drama: a beautiful defendant; mention of possible sexual exploits; public debate as to the guilt or innocence of the accused; and a virtual parade of some of the most noted and eloquent lawyers of the day. Plus, it was free entertainment. No doubt a number of the attendees traveled many hours by horse and buggy to observe the "really big show," and they were not disappointed.

The prosecution team of lawyers was headed up by Tom Watson, acting in place of the Solicitor-General. The actual Solicitor-General, O. H. Rogers was unable to attend due to "a painful rising on his face."[6] Some reports stated that the prosecution did not offer a motive for the killing, but others reported that robbery may have been the motive. Watson tried to prove that McCauley's appointment with Elvira was pre-arranged, as the guard dog was apparently put inside the house to prevent his barking upon McCauley's arrival. Watson made the point that the room where the killing took place was not Elvira's room and that she had no business there. Also, he suggested that the shotgun was already cocked, because had it not been, McCauley would have heard the noise of a cocking gun and been warned.

The love letters, supposedly written by Elvira Ivey to Jack McCauley played a significant role in the trial for voluntary manslaughter, and were the source of lengthy bantering back and forth between the prosecution and defense as to their admissibility. The letters, which were forty-five or so in number, were "most endearing" in their language, and contained wording that must have been scandalous for a young unmarried woman to send to a married man. As was expected, the defense attorneys objected to their admissibility, as they were not dated, addressed to or signed by anyone, with the one exception.

James Norris, the uncle of Sol Jones, (who served as Jones' advocate throughout his "troubles") testified in the commitment trial as well as the manslaughter trial of Elvira Ivey, concerning the infamous letters. Norris served as a witness for the State to help prove the letters were indeed written by Elvira. Norris claimed that while at a party in 1879 (five years prior), Elvira wrote him a note stating that her horse had gotten loose and she asked him to take her home. Norris also claimed that he had seen Elvira write a song ballad as well as some other writing. On this basis, he claimed to be able to identify her handwriting.

---

[6] The *Sandersville Herald* (Sandersville, Ga.), 15 May, 1885.

For some reason, Mr. Norris was criticized for his manner of testifying, but no details were offered in the press. After his testimony, the Court allowed about ten of the letters into evidence. The prosecution claimed that "if one of the letters were genuine, they all were."

After initially denying that she had written the letters, Elvira admitted that some of the letters were genuine, but claimed that they were written to Sol Jones and not to Jack McCauley. The prosecution pointed out that components of the letters showed they were *not* written to Sol Jones; in addition, Jones denied that they were written to him and went on to state that he had destroyed all letters he had received from Elvira.

Mrs. Frances McCauley, the widow of the murdered victim, also appeared in court "heavily veiled with the deepest black."[7] She testified that the letters were in her husband's possession before his death.

Tom Watson, in his arguments to the jury, pointed out that women are indeed capable of murder, as opposed to popular opinion. Watson cited several famous female murderers from world history and two from Georgia history...one of those being none other than Susan Eberhart.

The details of the trial of Elvira Ivey in Jefferson County Superior Court were recounted by a reporter for The *Augusta Chronicle*, in their 20 May, 1885 edition, as follows:

"LOUISVILLE, GA., May 18. - One of the most important cases that has been tried in the section of Georgia is that of the State vs. Elvira Ivey, charged with the

---

[7] The *Abbeville Messenger* (Abbeville, S. C.), 27 May, 1885.

murder of Jack McCauley. On last Thursday evening the case was called in Jefferson Superior Court, Judge Carswell presiding.

"The defendant came into court from jail and presented as attractive an appearance as is ever shown by a criminal at the bar. She has a handsome and pretty face, is youthful and attractive. The only marked features of her face are, a large chin and a bold, prominent eye. She was prettily dressed in a dress trimmed with delicate crimson and on her head she wore a light straw hat crowned with a crimsoned plume. [It was reported that part of the time Elvira held her infant on her lap.] She took her seat by her counsel, Messrs. Cain and Polhill, Gamble and Hunter and Hon. W. D. Tutt, of Augusta, who was her leading counsel in the case. The State was represented by the Solicitor pro tem. W. L. Phillips, and Hon. Thos. E. Watson, of McDuffie county. Both sides answered ready, a jury was soon empanelled and the great trial began.

"Mr. Watson conducted the prosecution and Mr. Gamble examined the witnesses on behalf of the defense. For two days the court was occupied with the evidence for the State. During that time there was many a tilt between counsel over points of law, admissibility of testimony and competency of witnesses. These debates between counsel were animated, spicy and sometimes eloquent, Messrs, Tutt, Gamble and Cain arguing for the defense, Mr. Watson replying for the State. Judge Carswell's rulings were prompt, and his bearing upon the bench decidedly fair and dignified.

"The case made was substantially this; McCauley and Miss Ivey have been intimate for years; McCauley a married man with two children, Miss Ivey unmarried. A great number of letters were written by Miss Ivey to McCauley; they spoke of assignations, appointed places of meeting, referred to her pregnant condition, and gave a vivid picture of the trouble which this criminal intimacy was bringing upon them. Mrs. McCauley knew of this correspondence, and finally separated from her husband because of it.

"A short time before the killing a negro man, Guss Hobbs, carried a letter from McCauley to Miss Ivey, and also bore him an answer. The letter claimed to be that one introduced, though not in any manner identified by the witness. It told him (McCauley) to come to her Tuesday night after the first Sunday, [This was the sole place that Tuesday night was mentioned, so perhaps this was an error by the reporter.]…described what window he must come to, and declared her willingness to elope with him, and said she would hand him her clothes out of the window, alluded to the separation between man and wife, and contained the remarkable sentence, 'You have told falsehoods enough on me to send your soul to hell.'

"On the Friday night after the first Sunday in December, McCauley went to the peculiar window now described, and was fatally shot by Miss Ivey. As to how the homicide was committed there was no evidence but her confession, as stated before the coroner's inquest. …

"The defendant having introduced no testimony, the case was opened for the defendant by Rodger M. Gamble, Esq., in a speech of one hour and forty minutes length, logical, forcible and effective. He was followed by Hon. T. E. Watson for the State in a two hours speech. Mr. Watson's speech was powerful and effective, and it seemed at its conclusion that the fate of the defendant was fixed. It was now the hour of 12½ at night. The jury had been confined to the court house for two days and had been sitting continuously from 9 o'clock in the morning till 12 ½ at night. Hon. W. D. Tutt at this hour began to address the jury. He commenced by begging the jury to consider that his client was a stranger, and that although they were tired and worn out with investigation, he begged for her a patient hearing. He spoke for half an hour, when Judge Carswell concluded to adjourn the court until next morning.

"At 9 o'clock Saturday morning Mr. Tutt resumed his speech, and for two hours he reviewed the testimony against his client and contended that if the letters were genuine – filled as they were with the most ardent love and affection – there could have been no motive for the deed; and also contended that McCauley went to the window for the purpose of abducting the defendant, and that she acted under the fears of a reasonable person – that a felony was about to be perpetrated upon her, and was, therefore justifiable. He closed in the following appeal in behalf of her aged mother who sat by her side and many eyes in the court room were moistened by this touching appeal:

Closing arguments by Col. W. D. Tutt follow:

" 'And now, gentlemen, I am done. I have done all that I could to demonstrate to you the innocence of this poor unfortunate woman. All of my zeal and all of the energy of my nature has been given to her defense, and now I must surrender her life and liberty into your tender keeping. I wish I knew what else to say that would remove any lingering doubt you may have in your minds of the innocence of her who stands charged with this awful crime. God knows I covet no man's gold, or silver, or jewels, or horses; but I do covet more than the miser covets glittering gold the eloquence which some men have, that I might to-day not only overpower your reason, but steal away your hearts and make them throb and palpitate, and glow with the pulsations of sympathy and God-given mercy towards this friendless and forlorn captive to-day. Oh! for an eloquence that would melt your hearts and calm them to dissolve in tender compassion and pity for this poor old heart-broken mother as she sits here and begs you in accents known only to a mother's loving heart to give back to her, to her loving arms, the

life of her debauched, dishonored, but still dearly loved daughter to-day. Oh! gentlemen, open your hearts to her gentle pleadings to-day. Thank God there is more genuine eloquence in a single pearly tear drop as it courses down the furrowed cheeks than there would or could be in all of the orators of the world. Thank God that while Moses maybe slow of speech, and stammer out with constrained accent the burning words of deliverance, there is in these loving tear drops which flow from an anguished heart, an Aaron which will plead eloquently. And withered by this blasting scorn of the cruel world, now in the supreme moment of her life's greatest trial, she twines the tendrils of a mother's love about her and will not give her up. Yes, here she is today, gentlemen, with the same devotion which characterized her when her daughter was pure and spotless. Here she stands, her mother's heart still yearning over her unfortunate darling, and she implores you by the memories of the past – as you remember the devotion of your own fond mother, by the contingencies of the future as they speak to you of what fate may possibly have in store for some of your own daughters – to soften and assuage the grief of this poor heart and restore her daughter to her loving arms once more. May God help you by your verdict to stifle her groans, to soothe her sorrow, to dry her tears and pour the glad oil of consolation into her grief-stricken heart.' "

"The Judge then delivered an able and exhaustive charge of about three-fourths of an hour, and the jury retired, and after four hours of deliberation they filed into the court room and returned the following verdict: 'We, the jury, find the defendant guilty of voluntary manslaughter.'

"Whereupon the Judge sentenced the prisoner to five years in the penitentiary. The counsel for the defense immediately filed a bill for a new trial upon thirteen grounds, two of which were: 1st, Because the Judge during the argument of the case left the court room; and, 2d: Because the Court re-charged the jury without the presence of the defendant, she being at that time in jail."

The jury, which had been boarded at the Central Hotel during the trial, was said to have initially stood "ten for acquittal and two for conviction."

It was said by a Washington D. C. newspaper, that "the feeling against hanging a woman was so strong that it was an easy matter to secure a new trial." However, this was not correct. Well, it was correct that the feeling was strong against hanging a woman in Georgia; but, as Elvira was sentenced to five years in the penitentiary on the charge of voluntary manslaughter, the possibility of hanging was not a factor when she gained a new trial.

After her conviction, while waiting for a new trial, Elvira was released on $1,500 bond. Five months later, in October of 1885, the criminal trial for seduction of Sol Jones was finally held in Warren County Superior Court, with Judge Samuel Lumpkin presiding. This was the culmination of a protracted legal battle, going back several years. All prior attempts to settle this matter were unsuccessful. Once again, the battle of the "legal Titans" played out in court; Tutt vs. Watson. No doubt Tom Watson, having "won" in the case of Elvira for manslaughter against Tutt, was eager to chalk up another victory against his legal nemesis.

In the trial for seduction, Elvira was the main witness for the State, and as she had just been convicted of voluntary manslaughter of her married lover, no doubt she was not viewed as especially credible. Though Watson in defense of his client Jones tried to prove that Elvira had been "ruined" before her alleged seduction by Jones, Judge Lumpkin did not allow this testimony because "the witnesses could not swear positively that this conduct was before the alleged seduction."[8] Elvira's testimony was impeached and proven to have contradictory statements. Therefore, the jury only debated for ten or fifteen minutes and found Sol Jones "not guilty."

The new trial of Elvira Ivey for manslaughter was initially scheduled for the next term of Jefferson County Superior Court in November of 1885, but had to be postponed due to the sickness of Mrs. Frances McCauley, the widow of the murder victim. The next term of Superior Court was held in May of 1886, but once again the trial was postponed – no explanation was given in the press. The case was also not heard in the November 1886 session; no explanation was given in the press for this either. When the May of 1887 session of Superior Court rolled around, Elvira did not appear and reportedly forfeited her bond. However, the *Atlanta Constitution* reported that, "Elvira Ivey, the Jefferson County murderess, through a fortunate attack of the measles, has secured another continuance of her case." Presumably she did not actually forfeit her bond due to this medical reason.

In the November 1887 term of Jefferson Superior Court, Elvira would finally get her day in court, to see if her legal team could win an acquittal for the charge of voluntary manslaughter. This was almost three years after the murder of Jack McCauley. By this time, Judge Carswell, the presiding judge in her initial trial, had been replaced by Judge J. K. Hines. It was most difficult to seat a jury, due to the immense amount of publicity concerning this case. Several panels were exhausted, and after several hours, only eleven jurors were seated. The Court resorted to sending bailiffs out in the country to hunt up jurors, as those in the town of Louisville attending court were rejected, having heard about the case or having formed an opinion on the case.

---

[8] The *Augusta Chronicle* (Augusta, Ga.), 17 Oct., 1885.

On her retrial for manslaughter, Tom Watson chose to not be involved in the prosecution. It was said that after reading the letters in Elvira's initial trial, Watson developed feelings of sympathy for her and did not wish to participate in the case. It is also of note that nowhere in the press does it indicate that Col. Tutt was involved in her retrial, so one must wonder if Watson also "passed" on this legal proceeding, as it did not offer an opportunity to spar with Tutt. As Watson was not a Solicitor at the time of the initial trial, but stepped in when Solicitor General Rogers had some kind of boil on his face, it would not be far-fetched to speculate that the skilled Watson was brought in just to do battle with the equally skilled Tutt; and that Watson's presence was not needed in the retrial. This is purely speculation.

In the retrial, Elvira was represented by J. W. Polhill and R. L. Gamble Jr., and the State was represented by Solicitor O. H. Rogers. The now infamous "letters" along with other evidence included in her initial trial were ruled inadmissible by the court in her retrial, which made for briefer proceedings. In her initial trial, the jury debated five hours; in her retrial, the jury returned the verdict of "not guilty" after only a few minutes. Just as in her initial trial, there were immense crowds of people attending Elvira's retrial. It was reported by one source that at her first trial, when she was found guilty of voluntary manslaughter and sentenced to five years in the penitentiary, the community seemed satisfied with the verdict. Other sources stated the public sentiment was in her favor at her initial trial, and that many felt she would be acquitted. However, upon her retrial when a verdict of "not guilty" was announced, there was great satisfaction and loud cheers by the large crowd. Actually, two of the most enthusiastic cheerleaders were fined $5 by the Court for their outbursts; these two being an Uncle of Miss Ivey from Warren County, (possibly her Uncle Tom), as well as a "quiet citizen of Jefferson County," who was not named.

There was a bit of excitement after the verdict in the retrial of Elvira; it was reported that one or more of the jurors in the retrial sat on the initial jury. It was later refuted in the press that the jurors mentioned, Mr. J. M. Perdue and Mr. L. R. Perdue were indeed *not* on the initial jury, so the sensational matter of the trials of Miss Elvira Ivey was finally put to rest.

Sometime after her acquittal in November of 1887, Elvira moved to nearby Washington County, in the area of Tennille, Georgia, and married James R. Barron and had three children. As there is no further mention of Elvira in the press, one can presume she settled in to family life and the "escapades" of her youth were behind her.

Perhaps William W. Brewton, in his 1926 book, "The Life of Thomas E. Watson," said it best:

Elvira "was acquitted, married a respectable farmer and never gained any more notoriety."

Just My Opinion

"Oh what a tangled web we leave,

When first we practice to deceive;

But when we've practiced for a while,

How vastly we improve our style."

(Sir Walter Scott, adapted by J. R. Pope)

While researching this story from over 130 years ago, it was my constant observation that the facts surrounding the case, and the participants' version of the facts did not seem to reconcile on any level. Most often with such stories of murder and cover-up, there may be one or perhaps a few participants that do not tell the truth. At the end of the day with this story, it is possible that *almost all* the participants were untruthful. One must remember that lying and deceit was the "order of the day" when illicit affairs were on the menu, and that avoidance of legal punishment, especially by hanging, was a strong motivator. With the overabundance of lies in this story, it truly is hard to make heads or tails of the details.

Who may have been the party that placed the obscene placards about Elvira? Initially I wondered if a woman (perhaps the wife of Sol. Jones or Mrs. Jack McCauley) may have done "the deed." Women sometimes like to do that sort of thing. But as it would have required a buggy ride of several hours from Warren to Jefferson County, it is unlikely a woman made such a trip by herself to nail posters to church doors, etc. Perhaps James Norris could have been involved; it was established that he was active in trying to clear the name of his nephew, Sol. Jones and was willing to go to great lengths to make that happen.

It seems absurd that James Norris recognized Elvira's handwriting from over five years prior, when he testified to that point in court. His credibility was must have been brought into question, and he was criticized for his manner of testimony. It seems very unlikely that a young woman would write a letter to an older man at a party, if she needed a ride home; unless of course, Elvira was making a "play" for him as well around the time of the "beginning of her troubles" when she was coming of age.

Why were none of the supposed letters from Elvira to Jack McCauley signed, with the single exception of the one which incriminated her in the murder? It would be expected *not* to sign or address love letters when one is involved in an illicit affair; and of course as they used a courier and not the United States Postal Service, no names were necessary. So, why was the one particular letter signed, not only once, but twice, in different inks? It would seem that someone wished to insure that Elvira was fingered in the murder, and possibly signed her name…but of course, if it was already signed once, why again? And wouldn't the party know it would appear to have been tampered with by using different ink? The wife of Jack McCauley (after the murder) was witnessed as getting the letters out of a locked drawer, the key hanging on the mantle. One would presume if she knew where the letters were after the murder, she knew where they were before the murder as well. It was stated in the press that she knew about the letters from Elvira to her husband prior to his murder…the letters possibly prompting her to leave her husband. Would Mrs. McCauley have wanted to insure that Elvira was known to be the author of the letters? I would think so; no doubt any wife would harbor great ill-will (I'm being kind) against her husband's lover.

It is somewhat bizarre that Elvira, at some point in the trial, confessed to writing some of the letters, but insisted at least some were forgeries. Then, she suggested that they were written to Sol. Jones, when clearly the contents did not seem to reconcile with that suggestion. When Sol Jones denied the letters presented at the trial were written to him, (claiming that he destroyed all of Elvira's letters), he opened himself up to the acknowledgment of a relationship with Elvira. One wonders if this portion of his testimony came up in Jones' trial for seduction.

Is it possible that the one letter that was signed was indeed a forgery? The contents of that letter seem to present a strange dichotomy; on one hand, Elvira seemed to make plans to elope with the man she loved, but on the other hand accused him of such lies that he would go "to hell." Then, she went on to question whether they would ever live together peacefully, but made plans to do so anyway.

Which brings up another question; if Elvira did indeed write the letters, what kind of lies did Elvira accuse Jack McCauley of telling on her? My only thought is - if folks knew Elvira was pregnant, it may have been rumored that Jack McCauley was the father. *So*, McCauley may have, in attempt to deny his involvement, stated that Elvira was pregnant by someone else – perhaps Sol Jones? McCauley may have told such lies to try to keep his wife from finding out the truth about the baby.

After confessing to the murder at the coroner's inquest, why did Elvira disappear? I do not believe her Uncle Tom Ivey, in his explanation that he wished to arrange her surrender in private to avoid the embarrassment of a commitment trial. The "embarrassment train" already left the station when speaking of Elvira. Perhaps the family planned for Elvira to confess, then escape to "wherever" and live out her days in obscurity. In that era, Texas seemed to be a popular destination for anyone wishing to "escape their past" and start a new life.

Even "non-lawyer" types know that to prosecute a case of murder, the attorney needs to at least suggest a plausible motive. However, in the case of Elvira, the State either failed to offer a motive, or suggested robbery as a possible motive, depending on whose report was accurate. The letters that the State fought so hard to introduce into evidence actually presented a dilemma for Tom Watson; the letters presented a loving relationship between Elvira and Jack, but they would also help "shoot down" Elvira's explanation that she did not know Jack, which would help establish her as a liar. Col. Tutt, who fought to keep the letters from being introduced into evidence, also had a dilemma: the letters would help establish the loving relationship between Elvira and McCauley, which would make it hard for Watson to suggest a motive; but again, they would establish that Elvira, his client, was a liar. What a conundrum!

It was suggested in the press as a possible motive that perhaps Elvira and her family lured McCauley to her brother's house to rob him; but, as the money was still on his person after the murder, that theory did not seem to hold water. Why would you lure an unarmed man with a large amount of money to your window, with the intent to rob him, then shoot him and not take the money? Nowhere was it reported that in any of the letters supposedly written by Elvira contained the request for McCauley to bring a sum of money to her residence. The prosecution did offer as a possible theory that Elvira expected McCauley to come to her window that night, and put the guard dogs in the house to prevent their barking in alarm. But of course, she would have put the dogs up if she planned to rob McCauley, just as if she expected to run off with McCauley. This information seemed more like an explanation of events, than the suggestion of a motive. In addition, if Elvira's family was "in on it," the plan being to rob McCauley, why would she put the guard dogs in the house? That act indicates that Elvira wished McCauley's presence to not awaken the other family members, which supports the theory that she was running off with McCauley.

Much was made over the fact that Jack McCauley brought a single horse to Elvira's brother's house the night he was murdered. Those that claimed McCauley was there to run off with Elvira could not explain why he came on a single horse, and did not bring one for Elvira…noting that this seemed strange. Tom Watson, in his letter to the editor, pointed out that it would seem even stranger that McCauley was there to abduct her and brought a single horse. However, Watson made this suggestion at the time he was representing Sol Jones for seduction, *before* he became involved in the prosecution of Elvira for murder. It is my belief McCauley was there to elope with Elvira, and brought a single horse, period. The fact that Jack McCauley did not bring a gun, but only a pocket knife, brings into question the suggestion that he was there to kidnap Elvira.

Elvira's version that she did not know the identity of the man at the window; that he offered her $1,500 to run off with him; that he threatened her if she did not run away with him; and that she threw out a few belongings and then shot him in self-defense also seems ludicrous. How was McCauley going to "blow her brains out" when he didn't even have a gun? Perhaps the words "blow your brains out" were spoken that night, but by the person who actually did the deed, and *not* Jack McCauley. Then, Elvira went on to suggest that perhaps she *did* know his identity, and tried to persuade him to not run away, as he had a duty to his wife and children. Again, ludicrous.

A side-note of interest: Elvira claimed that the unidentified party at her window "jerked open the window" before he began the threats, etc. It was specifically noted that the window was six and a half feet from the ground. This would have been an old wooden farmhouse with double-hung windows. Nowhere is there any mention of a ladder in the crime scene. And of course, the window would have been closed on a chilly December night. Elvira may have jerked open the window while standing inside, but it would seem impossible that someone standing outside on the ground could have done what Elvira claimed.

It seems apparent to anyone reading the story of Elvira Ivey that she did not pull the trigger and murder Jack McCauley, (with the exception of two of her attorneys, who believed she *was* guilty). Interestingly, it was reported that the jury initially voted 10 for acquittal and 2 for conviction. Most in the community believed she was innocent of murder, and no doubt observers noticed clues in the mannerisms of the parties that led them to believe Elvira was covering for someone. The likely parties were suggested to be her father or her brother. This would make sense, in light of the case of Susan Eberhart. Any woman in Georgia after the Eberhart case knew that almost certainly she would *not* be hanged for murder, and possibly would receive a light sentence, perhaps five years or less. Men, however, were still being hanged for murder after the Eberhart case. If Elvira and the guilty party, as well as the other family members present, discussed "what to do" after the murder, it is almost certain that Elvira was either asked or volunteered to confess, in order to save her father or brother from hanging.

So, who was Elvira covering for? I suggest *not* for her father. He was known to be a good Christian family man, and I cannot imagine a father of that type allowing his possibly pregnant daughter to sit in jail, stand trial and go to prison to save his own neck. But, I can imagine such a man allowing his daughter to take the blame if it meant his son would be saved from the gallows. It would be perhaps a case of the "lesser of two evils."

I can imagine the tragic murder occurred something like this:

Elvira brought embarrassment and shame to her family through her promiscuity and pregnancy out of wedlock. Her brother allowed her to come to his house to escape the lewd and obscene posters and "talk" about his sister, as well as to give birth to her illegitimate baby. Unfortunately her reputation followed her to Jefferson County, bringing humiliation on her brother and his wife, (who, by the way, were good members of Reedy Creek Baptist Church). When Jack McCauley's wife left him and took the children, he realized his "life as he knew it" was over. So, he made plans to run off to Texas with Elvira and start over, taking a sizeable sum of money with him. As Elvira and Jack knew her family would not approve of their plans, they plotted to carry out flight in secret, in the dead of night, hoping to be well on their way before they were found to be missing. On the night of the murder, the brother was awakened by a noise, presumably the opening of a window and possibly the barking of the dogs inside the house; found pregnant Elvira in the process of sneaking out the window to run away with a married lover; got into a heated argument with Jack McCauley; lost his temper and shot and killed him. Elvira's brother John Marion Ivey had no doubt finally just had enough; one must remember that Elvira's "bad behavior" had been going on for about seven years. Also, Elvira was in the midst of the protracted legal battle with Sol. Jones, and to have the entire community now know that she was pregnant and eloped with a married man…well, that would be hard for anyone to bear.

As this murder occurred in the era before fingerprints, forensics and lie-detectors; none of those tools were available for use in determining guilt. There was a confession (by Elvira) and no other witnesses. So, apparently after Elvira was acquitted, no one was ever charged with the murder of Jack McCauley. It does seem significant that John, Elvira's brother, always seemed to suffer from some kind of unresolved "guilt" after the murder, as he often fell to his knees and prayed at the end of rows he plowed from that point forward.

As for the closing argument at Elvira's trial by Col. W. D. Tutt; I have to smile a bit when reading his remarks, as he repeatedly seems to express to the jury that his greatest desire in life was – to be an eloquent speaker, with the clear implication that he was *not* an eloquent speaker. Based on almost every news account of Col. W. D. Tutt, he was a noted attorney with a statewide reputation for one thing: his *eloquence* as a speaker!

When the eloquent and noted attorney, Col. W. D. Tutt, saw his client Elvira appear in Jefferson County Superior Court wearing a straw hat with a crimson plume feather, holding her illegitimate baby on her lap, this certainly came as no surprise to Tutt. All competent lawyers coach their clients before they appear in court, especially those charged with murder. I suggest that Col. Tutt knew there was no way he could present Elvira as an innocent young lady, falsely accused of sexual improprieties. Therefore, he chose to present her as what she was – a promiscuous and beautiful young woman, but with a catch; her Mother appeared as the sympathetic figure, crying and sorrowful over the moral failures of her beloved daughter. Tutt even went one step further, and tried to make the jury think of their own dear mothers, their own moral failures as well as perhaps the moral failures of their own daughters. His strategy seemed to work with the gallery, but the jury still found Elvira "guilty."

By the time Elvira was re-tried for voluntary manslaughter a little over two years later, the feelings of the community were more sympathetic toward her and they did not wish for her to go to prison. Public sentiment was - that she did *not* commit the murder, and folks also knew she had a young child. And just perhaps, the beautiful Miss Elvira Ivey had changed her ways…

Lessons Learned

For me to give the amount of time and effort necessary to research and publish a book requires a compelling reason and a lesson learned. In the case of the story of Elvira Ivey, it was not merely to tell a salacious and sordid story from long ago. It would never be my desire to bring to light the moral failures of another's family, knowing that my family has moral failures as well, frankly, just like everyone's family. When recounting a story from history such as the one of Elvira Ivey, as well as the one of Susan Eberhart, it is helpful to look at the "themes" of the story to give direction to the "lessons learned."

While there are a number of similarities in the stories of Susan and Elvira, there are stark contrasts as well. Susan and Elvira were both young women about age 20 when they found themselves charged with murder; both were involved in illicit love affairs; and both lived in the period just after the Civil War in rural areas of Georgia. That is about where the similarities end. The themes found in the tragedy of Susan Eberhart are poverty, ignorance, mental illness, justice and mercy. There does not seem to be overlap of the themes of Susan Eberhart's story with that of Elvira Ivey.

"The consequences of physical beauty" and "the wages of sin," would best describe the events described in the story of Elvira Ivey. Though most if not all women desire physical beauty, at least in the case of Elvira, that wish granted was a mixed blessing. Because of her extreme beauty, Elvira attracted the attention of men at a very early age, before she was mature enough to handle the results of that attention. This led to her ruined reputation, which in that era, was considerably more damaging than in our time. Her beauty obviously led to Jack McCauley's obsession with her, to the extent he was willing to give up his wife and children in pursuit of Elvira, ultimately leading to his tragic death. I suppose one could say that on the "plus" side of Elvira's beauty, would be the special treatment she received by law enforcement, in the court system and most likely by the public at large. One cannot help but wonder if Elvira had been a rather plain girl, would her story have had a very different ending?

As for the concept of "sin" in Elvira's story, we have *all* sinned and fallen short of the Glory of God. The Bible states that fact, and reality bears it out. None of us are blameless; it is only through the Amazing Grace of God that we are able to stand in His presence. Elvira's sins were more public, perhaps, than ours, but no greater… if you believe as I do, that sin is sin and all equally unacceptable in the eyes of God.

My husband frequently quotes in his sermons, "Sin always takes you further, keeps you longer, and costs you more than you ever expect." This was especially true in the story of Elvira Ivey. I am sure that when Solomon Jones first locked eyes with Elvira Ivey, he never expected to end up in court charged with seduction; have his reputation drug through the mud of his home county; or to be a witness in the murder trial of his former lover, who was charged in the death of his rival for her affections. Likewise, Jack McCauley, upon first locking eyes with Elvira Ivey, never expected to lose his wife and children in the breakup of his marriage, or to be murdered at the window of his lover. As for Elvira Ivey: certainly when she engaged in illicit love affairs, she never expected to give birth to an illegitimate child; have her family caught up in scandal; or have her reputation ruined by the publicity of placards and gossip. Nor did she ever expect to end up in court, charging her lover with seduction or charged *with* the murder of another lover.

"No man sins to himself alone." This story presents a striking illustration of the devastating effects of sin not only on the persons actively involved, but their families, friends and even their descendants. The stories of Elvira Ivey and the murder of Jack McCauley have been passed down for generations, and make for a most negative piece of family lore. The wife of Jack McCauley and his children must have suffered terribly due to his actions and his murder brought about by those actions. In a similar way, Elvira's parents and family also suffered from this terrible tragedy. Even Solomon Jones' family suffered as a result of his actions, though he was found not guilty in court.

In the Bible, Solomon, the wisest man that ever lived, shared words in Proverbs that seem applicable to this story: *"Charm is deceptive, and beauty is fleeting; but a woman who fears the Lord is to be praised."* Solomon goes on to tell the consequences of a man drawn into an inappropriate sexual relationship: *"With persuasive words she led him astray; she seduced him with her smooth talk. All at once he followed her like an ox going to the slaughter, like a deer stepping into a noose till an arrow pierces his liver, like a bird darting into a snare, little knowing it will cost him his life."*

But there is good news at the end of this tragic tale; there can be forgiveness of sins and redemption for anyone wishing to receive the good and gracious gift of salvation through a belief in Jesus Christ, and acceptance of Him as Lord and Savior. The gift has been offered to us all…you, me and Miss Elvira Ivey.

The Rest of the Story

Hon. Thomas E. Watson (1856-1922): Sketch from website of The Watson-Brown Foundation:

"Thomas E. Watson was born September 5, 1856, two miles outside Thomson, Georgia. After attending Mercer and then reading law, Watson was admitted to the Bar and returned to Thomson in 1877 to begin a successful law practice. He served in the Georgia House of Representatives in 1882, the U. S. House of Representatives from 1890-1892 and the U. S. Senate from 1920 until his death in 1922. Watson emerged as the leader of the Southern Populists soon after his election to Congress. He was nominated in 1896 for Vice President on the same ticket with William Jennings Bryan. He ran for President on the same ticket in 1904 and 1908. Although Watson held political office for just five of his 66 years, he dominated Georgia's political scene for more than 25 years. In addition to being a statesman and the premier trial lawyer of Georgia in his day, Watson was a prolific writer. He authored a two volume history of France, biographies of Napoleon, Thomas Jefferson and Andrew Jackson, and numerous other books, pamphlets and published speeches. Watson published and edited his weekly newspaper, The Jeffersonian, and his monthly Watson's Magazine for more than a decade."

Thom. Watson's home "Hickory Hill," in Thomson, Georgia, is a National Historic Landmark. The Watson-Brown Foundation, named in honor of Thomas E. Watson and J. J. Brown, exists to support education and preserve the history of the American South.

Judge Reuben Walker Carswell (1839-1889): Judge Carswell was the presiding judge in the first manslaughter case of Elvira Ivey in Jefferson County Superior Court. His biography quoted from "Find-A-Grave" website, is as follows: "Civil War Confederate Officer. Prior to the American Civil War this native of Jefferson County, Georgia was an attorney. He graduated from Emory College in Oxford, Georgia, and after reading law under the tutelage of future Confederate General Ambrose Ransom Wright was accepted to the Georgia Bar. Further, he was active in state politics and was elected to represent his community in the Georgia State Legislature (1858-1860). In the early days of the war, he along with other volunteers, massed to organize the 'Jefferson Guards.' ... [After the Civil War] his remaining days passed in Louisville, Georgia, where he renewed his legal practice. In the year 1881, he was appointed judge of the 'Superior Courts of the Middle Circuit' of Georgia. He died at the age of 51-years old on January 11, 1889." Judge Carswell is buried in the Louisville City Cemetery, Louisville, Georgia.

Col. Rev. James Stapleton (1824-1888): After having lived his entire life in Jefferson County, Ga., as a teacher, farmer, merchant, Civil War soldier, and state legislator, James Stapleton spent his final years as a circuit preacher, chronicling the daily events in his diary. My Great-Grandfather James continued to make daily entries in his journal until his last entry on January 23, 1888, just a few weeks before his death on Feb. 21, 1888. His entry on December 31, 1887 was as follows:

"Saturday. All up, but I am quite feeble. One year ago I had but little hope that I would live to see the close of another year – But the good Lord has seen fit to preserve me, and I am still alive, but nothing more than a skeleton. Thousands

have died during the present that were young, stout and strong, while the old and afflicted have been spaired. Gods ways is not mans ways..."

The marker for James Stapleton is in the Baptist Church Cemetery in Stapleton, Ga., the town which was named in his honor in 1885.

Judge James Kollock "J. K." Hines (1852-1932): Judge Hines presided over the second trial for manslaughter of Elvira Ivey in Jefferson County Superior Court, in which she was acquitted. Hines was raised in Sandersville, Ga. on his father's plantation, "Whitehall." While practicing law, he was considered an expert in the field of criminal law. He went on to become a Justice of the Georgia State Supreme Court. Hines died in 1932 and is buried in Westview Cemetery in Atlanta.

Judge Samuel Lumpkin (1848-1902): Judge Lumpkin presided over the trial of Solomon Jones for seduction in Warren County Superior Court. He was born in Oglethorpe County, Ga., and was the grand-nephew of Joseph Henry Lumpkin, the first Supreme Court Justice of the State of Georgia. After serving as a Solicitor General and Superior Court Justice of the Northern Judicial District, Samuel Lumpkin went on to become an Associate Justice of the Supreme Court of Georgia in 1891. He is buried in the Lumpkin family cemetery in Oglethorpe County, Ga.

Solomon Jones (1855 -1921): It would seem that, based on his obituary, Sol. Jones settled in to a rather normal life after his acquittal on the charge of seduction from Elvira Ivey. However, his life ended in a violent manner when he was about 65 years old. Sol. Jones engaged in an argument with his neighbor, Sam. G. Story, which resulted in Story shooting and killing Jones. Story was found guilty of murder, and sentenced to prison for 14 to 16 years. Both Sol.

Jones and Sam G. Story are buried in the cemetery of Sweetwater Baptist Church, near Thomson, Georgia.

Hon. W. D. Tutt (1838-1906):
Obituary printed in the *Lincoln Home Journal,* 10 May, 1906: "WILLIAM DUNCAN TUTT. Prominent Lawyer and Popular Citizen passes to Great Beyond. – On Monday afternoon at his home in this county, Col. William D. Tutt breathed his last. For Some years it has been apparent to Col. Tutt's friends that his health was declining, and his condition for the past few weeks has been such as to cause serious apprehension to those who were nearest to him, and warn them that his end was approaching, yet the news of his death came as a great blow to his wide circle of friends and caused universal and widespread sorrow wherever he was known.

"Col. Tutt was born and raised in this county but after his graduation from Emory College he entered upon the practice of law at Washington, Wilkes county. Later he returned to the county of his nativity and was called upon by the people among whom he was reared to serve them in the legislature, where he was recognized as one of the ablest members of that body. Subsequently he practiced his profession at Thomson, Augusta and Elberton, in all of which places he easily took first rank among the members of the bar. He also served this district in the state senate with signal ability. As a lawyer, Col. Tutt had few equals. His power before a jury was wonderful and he was recognized at the bar of Georgia.

"It was in a political convention also that his powers as an orator showed to advantage. Some years ago, when there was a stubborn deadlock in the state convention in Atlanta, Col. Tutt sprang into prominence by a speech which electrified the convention, and which led the late Henry W. Grady to refer to him as 'Plain Bill Tutt,' which name his friends ever afterwards delighted to call him.

"At the time of his death he was about 68 years old. His remains were interred in the cemetery at Pine Grove church on Tuesday afternoon, Ref. Author Maness performing the last rites."

Adam Ivey (1826 -1898): Adam Ivey, Elvira's Father, outlived his wife Louisa, and died in Washington County, Georgia. He is buried in the cemetery of the Sisters Baptist Church.

Louisa Cason Ivey (1829-1886): Louisa, the mother of Elvira, died in 1886, before Elvira was acquitted for the manslaughter of Jack McCauley. She is buried in the cemetery of Sisters Baptist Church in Sandersville, Georgia (Washington County). It would seem that Louisa and Adam, the parents of Elvira, moved to Washington County sometime after the trouble in Jefferson County with Elvira, possibly to be near one of their sons.

Fred T. Lockhart (1850-1907): Fred Tutt Lockhart was the son of Sarah Lockhart and Dr. George Manly Tutt– who was the half-brother of Col. W. D. Tutt. It was said that Fred's father "drank a lot," leading to his parent's divorce; after which Fred was adopted by his Grandfather Lockhart – thus the name of Fred Tutt Lockhart. Col. W. D. Tutt and Fred T. Lockhart were partners in the Augusta law firm, "Tutt & Lockhart," and both were attorneys for Elvira Ivey. Fred Lockhart was noted as a fine Christian man, and is buried in the Summerville Cemetery in Augusta, Ga.

Hon. Roger Lawson Gamble (1851-1912): Roger Gamble was a native of Louisville, Ga. and served as one of Elvira's defense attorneys in the manslaughter trial. He went on to become a Judge of the Middle Judicial Circuit. Gamble died in North Carolina, but is buried in the Louisville City Cemetery.

Hon. Hurst "Edward" Hunter (1853-1892): Edward Hunter was one of the defense attorneys for Elvira in her trial for manslaughter. A portion of his obituary, from an unknown newspaper, is posted on Ancestry.com website: "Louisville, Ga., March 15. – [Hunter] was adjunct professor of mathematics and civil engineering at the university of Athens,….Having a desire to study law he returned to his home in Louisville, where, after a thorough course of study under Judge J. G. Cain, he was admitted to the bar, of which profession he has been a conspicuous master." Edward Hunter died just short of his 39th birthday, and is buried in the Louisville City Cemetery.

Hon. James Granberry Cain (1835-1910): J. G. Cain, one of the defense attorneys in Elvira's manslaughter trial, was a native of Jefferson County and studied at Mercer University when it was located in Penfield, Ga. He then studied law at Sparta, Ga. and was admitted to the bar in 1856. He fought, and was wounded in the Civil War, rising to the rank of Lieutenant Colonel in the Confederate Army. In addition to practicing law, he went on to serve in the State Legislature and become a Judge. J. G. Cain is buried in the Louisville Cemetery. (Information from "Roster of Confederate Soldiers of Georgia 1861-1865 Military History," posted on Ancestry.com Website.)

Hon. Joseph Hamilton Polhill (1842-1927): Joseph Polhill was one of the team of attorneys for the defense of Elvira in her manslaughter trial. Polhill was a native of Jefferson County, fought for the Confederacy in the Civil War, served in the State Legislature and is buried in the Louisville City Cemetery.

James Conquest Cross Black "J. C. C." (1842-1930): J. C. C. Black was one of Elvira's team of attorneys. Mr. Black was from Kentucky, fought for the Confederacy in the Civil War, and practiced law in Augusta, GA. He was elected to the Georgia Legislature in 1873-1877, and went on to be elected to the U. S. House of Representatives in 1893. He died in 1930 and is buried in the Magnolia Cemetery in Augusta, Ga.

Alexander B. McCauley (Dec. 23, 1875 – 1897): Alex was the son of Jack McCauley, and his father was murdered just a week or so before his ninth birthday. His younger sister Eva was only about six years old when her father was murdered. Tragically, Alex too was murdered at age 21 in Wilkes County, Ga. The following was taken from The Augusta Chronicle, 16 Nov., 1897: *"MURDER NEAR WASHINGTON – NEGRO SHOOTS YOUNG WHITE MAN AND MAKES HIS ESCAPE. – Washington, Nov. 15. (Special) – A young man named Alex McCauley was killed by a negro, Sim Thomas, last night at 8 o'clock on Mr. Dack Taylor's place, ten miles east of Washington. The killing was done just outside a negro house. No one was present at the time of the killing except the two men, and the cause of the killing is unknown. Mr. McCauley was about 20 years of age and well thought of. The negro ran away after shooting him. A reward of $25 has been offered for his capture."*

Alex and his mother Francis (the widow of Jack McCauley) are both buried in the Smyrna United Methodist Church Cemetery near Washington, Ga. His sister Eva McCauley Burdett lived to age 89, and is buried in in Ebenezer Cemetery in Wilkes County, Ga.

Elvira Ivey (1863-1939): Sancil Elvira Ivey moved to Tennille, Ga. in Washington County sometime after her trial. On January 3, 1889, she married James R. Barron, and later had three children: a son, Ivey Lee Barron, born 1891; a daughter, Mamie (or Amie?) Louise, born 1895; and Lena May, born 1899. After the death of her husband, she lived with her daughter in Macon, where she later died. Both Elvira and her husband James are buried in Zeta Cemetery in Tennille, Ga.

Andrew Jackson "Jack" McCauley (1848-1884): The burial place of Jack McCauley is unknown.

Appendix

Exhibit (1) Thomas E. Watson & W. D. Tutt

Excerpt from "Tom Watson, Agrarian Rebel" by C. Vann Woodward:

Chapter VII – *Agrarian Lawmaking*:

" 'Since the Convention of 1880 I had had a fixed determination to run for the Legislature this year,' wrote Watson in 1882…He did not believe there would have been any opposition had not his shooting scrape with W. D. Tutt brought on 'various obstacles.' …Feeling between Watson and Tutt had been brewing for over five years. The day Watson arrived in Thomson to begin his law practice in 1876 he was greeted at the railway station by loud guffaws provoked by a remark at his expense from Tutt. 'If I had my gun,' Watson told a friend, 'I would have shot him right there.' Although Tutt was several years his senior, and was already established as a highly successful lawyer, Watson's aggressive rise in the profession was not long in challenging Tutt's place of preeminence at the local bar. Watson's success appears to have been won largely at the expense of his rival. In the three and a half years preceding March, 1882, his 'Lawyer's Record Book' accounts for twenty-nine cases in which he and Tutt represented opposing interests, only twenty-two in which Tutt was not his opponent, and just one in which they collaborated. Many of these were criminal suits, in which popular excitement ran high, feelings were strained and taut, and rivalry bitter and personal. Watson was by far the more successful of the two in their clashes, and it was not but natural for the older man to resent the impertinence of an upstart's rivalry.

"...In March, 1881, Tom [Watson], his brother Julius, and Tutt were jointly indicted for 'carrying concealed weapons.' At the trial the following January the Watson brothers pleaded guilty, Tutt not guilty. The court fined each of the three twenty-five dollars. Serious trouble was expected almost any day now. The rivals had already clashed in two cases in March when Watson conceived the idea that Tutt had done him an injury by accepting a case in his absence that he thought should have been his. At a chance meeting in a law office in Thomson words were exchanged. Watson was insulting. Tutt struck him. Watson drew a gun and fired, striking Tutt, who had raised a chair before him, on the hand. Watson was disarmed, and the two were separated.

"On March 22 Watson was indicted for 'assault with intent to murder,' and only two days later appeared for trial before Judge Claiborne Snead. He had engaged, from the many who offered to defend him, three competent lawyers, among them, James C. C. Black, of Augusta. A jury was impaneled and sworn, and the case proceeded until the State closed. Then friends of both parties suggested a 'settlement.' Watson, apparently seeking vindication, 'opposed it bitterly and only gave in at the last moment upon condition that I should state my side of the case.' This done, Judge Snead withdrew the issue from the jury and ordered 'good cause having been shown, the said case be and is hereby settled.'"

****

Selection from "Reminiscences of Famous Georgians," by Lucian Lamar Knight, published 1907:

"The writer's first acquaintance with oratory in Georgia began far back in the seventies [1870s] when he used to accompany his grandfather to the Capitol during the long summer sessions of the State Legislature… Among the eloquent Georgians whose voices still ring in memory above the din of more than three decades the writer vividly recalls Fleming duBignon and Pope Barrow and W. D. Tutt and Lucius M. Lamar and Robert Falligant…. But scarcely inferior to duBignon was W. D. Tutt. If less classical he was more vehement; and at times he made the very walls tremble. Yet this intense orator who seemed to have caught some of the sparks from the anvil of Demosthenes, has been content to bury himself in the woods of North Georgia.

"Another vivid recollection brings to mind the electrical speech of Tom Watson in the famous gubernatorial convention of 1880. It was the most effective short speech which the writer has ever heard. The vast assemblage was intolerant of further outbursts of oratory, but when this slender youth took the floor and began to speak the most profound silence composed the hall. It mattered not that he supported one of the weaker candidates. He lifted the convention to the very highest pitch of enthusiasm."

****

Selection from "The Life of THOMAS E. WATSON" by William W. Brewton published 1926:

"A LITERARY ADDRESS:

"At the May term, 1885, of Jefferson Superior Court (Louisville, Georgia) Mr. Watson appeared in one of the most dramatic cases of his entire career, that of Elvira Ivey, a beautiful 20-year-old adventuress, indicted for the murder of Jackson McCauley, a married man, and her alleged lover. McCauley was shot to death with a shot-gun as he approached her bedroom window late at night.

"The unusual case as built up by the state's evidence was that McCauley had left his wife and two children because of an infatuation for Miss Ivey, and approached her window on the night of the killing in response to a letter from her, promising to go away with him. The text of this letter appeared in the newspapers. It had been delivered by hand and bore no name, the woman denying she wrote it. Testimony by persons claiming to know her handwriting was convincing that she did.

"Mr. Watson was engaged to prosecute the young woman. The Solicitor-General being ill, he prepared the case for the grand jury, W. L. Phillips acting as Solicitor General pro tem. On the trial there appeared by the defense, as chief counsel, the inevitable and brilliant W. D. Tutt, with whom were associated Messrs. Cain & Polhill and Gamble & Hunter.

"The defense offered nothing but Miss Ivey's statement which was, in brief, that about 2 o'clock on the night of the killing she was awakened by a knocking at her window; that on demanding who it was, a man's voice commanded her to get up and go with him; that if she consented he would give her $1,500, but if she refused he 'would blow her brains out'; that she handed the man a box of clothes, then seized a shot-gun and fired out the window without aim and without knowing who was there.

"Mr. Watson had entire control of shaping the state's case. It was that the young woman lured McCauley to her window, in conspiracy with her people to rob him, knowing he was to have $1,500 on his person, with which to elope, having promised to secure a divorce from his wife and marry her; that this plot was borne out by the circumstances of a late hour at night; a secluded place; failure of a fierce watch-dog to make any noise, indicating that he had been taken into the house; and failure of the old-fashioned hammer shot-gun to be heard when cocked, indicating it had been cocked in advance.

"Watson put all his power into his 2-hour argument delivered in a crowded courtroom at midnight, endeavoring to break the force of the fact that the defendant was a woman, the crux of which was: 'They claim a woman commits no such crime. Examples are to the contrary. In Georgia there were Kate Sothern and **Susan Eberhart**. In history, Lucretia Borgia, Fredegonda, Brunehilda, Jezebel, Beatrice Cenci.'

"Tutt concluded, but Miss Ivey was convicted of voluntary manslaughter, and Judge Carswell sentenced her to serve five years in the penitentiary. She later secured a new trial. Letters that had been interchanged between her and McCauley had aroused in Mr. Watson a sympathy for her. He did not appear against her in the second trial and she was acquitted, married a respectable farmer and never gained any more notoriety.

"In her statement to the jury she had accused one Solomon Jones of seducing her before she met McCauley. For this alleged offense Jones was indicted in Warren

County and in his case Watson, with James Whitehead, appeared for the defense, and Tutt, Joseph Pottle and Solicitor-General Howard for the state. Jones was acquitted."

****

"SOME RECOLLECTIONS OF WILLIAM D. TUTT."

(By THOS. E. WATSON); The *McDuffie Progress* (Thomson, Ga.), 8 August, 1913:

"There was a certain man by the name of Hamilton who crossed over into Georgia from the Carolina side of the River, and who straightway organized a band of robbers. I do not mean that he applied for a charter, took a corporate name, and asked Congress to 'protect' his infant industry. What I do mean is, that this man Hamilton undertook to earn a livelihood by plundering such of his fellow Christians as could not help themselves.

"Hamilton's methods were old-fashioned and crude, and the natural consequence was that he soon became entangled in the meshes of the Law – he and his amateur band. A young man from Lincoln County was charged with being one of these Hamiltonians; and, in his distress, this young man sent for his kinsman, W. D. Tutt, a lawyer then unknown to fame.

"I was a mere lad at the time, but I remember what a commotion it created in our good old Baptist-Methodist community, to awake to the fact that we had in our midst a real, live band of highwaymen, robbers, gangsters, bandits, brigands and land-pirates. Even the old folks quit talking about their rheumatisms and toothaches, to expatiate on this new variety of lawlessness.

"Col. Tutt came, saw and conquered. He was then in the prime of life. His face was ruddy, his form stalwart and erect; his manner confident, bold and magnetic. I have seldom seen a finer figure of *a man*. He made some speeches for his kinsman – in applying for *Habeas Corpus*, as I remember – and it was said that Toombs himself had never been more eloquent. In other words, Col. Tutt became the hero of the hour in McDuffie; the subject of admiring talk; and, soon afterwards, he had moved to Thomson to practice law.

"While I was down in Screven County teaching school and eating the bitter bread of poverty and discouragement, I heard from time to time that Col. Tutt was doing splendidly at the bar. He outclassed Paul Hudson, Juriah Casey and Henry Roney – his local competitors. His knowledge of the law was not greater than theirs, but he was far and away their master in debate, in cross-examination, in catchy speeches to the jury, and in the telling of apt anecdotes.

"On my return to my old home, in November 1876, I found Col. Tutt in full swing. He had made money, had invested it wisely, and was prospering in every way. He was taking a leading part in the Methodist church; was a factor in all local affairs; and later on, became the head of the movement which gave rise to our present High School. In McDuffie, Lincoln, Taliaferro, Columbia, Warren and Glasscock, Col. Tutt had one side of nearly every important law case – to say nothing of occasional employment in Wilkes, Elbert, Hancock, Jefferson and Richmond. His yearly income must have been large for that time – some $3,000 at least.

"Full of life, conscious of his strength, almost intoxicated by sudden success, Col. Tutt clashed into other lawyers with much gusto and frequency. He loved a rough and tumble fight, in the court house and on the stump, better than he did ham and eggs. I have seen him when he was at his best, and when he dominated his surroundings like a king. The common run of lawyers were "not in it," at all, when Col. Tutt had a case that appealed to him, and a crowded court-room that was boisterous with laughter and the buzz of admiration as he dealt blow after blow upon his opponents. His powers of ridicule were terrible: I have seen strong men cringe under the lash of his stinging wit, his withering sarcasm. Endowed with a giant's strength, he sometimes used it *like* a giant; and the victims suffered. But that is human nature: the same thing could be said of Ranse Wright, Robert Toombs and Ben Hill.

"This must have been the happiest period of the Colonel's life. To the west of the town, he had a beautiful home, on a farm that was increased from year to year by additional purchases of land. He kept regular office-hours in Thomson, riding horse-back, or walking in from his suburban home. He was a constant attendant at his church, and was often at ours, "on the other side of the railroad." He enjoyed the happiest relations with his beautiful wife, and his little boys – often speaking of how he would pass the time at the evening fireside by reading the novels of Charles Dickens. I thought then, and think now, that his home life was ideal.

"In a hotly-fought slander case in Taliaferro, Col. Tutt gained a victory that was all the talk, for months. I was at Liberty Hall soon afterwards, and Mr. Stephens mentioned it to me, as the local sensation. [Reference to Alexander H. Stephens, former Vice-President of the Confederacy, and his home in Crawfordville, Ga. named 'Liberty Hall.'] The Colonel was presented by his clients with a handsome souvenir of the case, and I presume his family still have it.

"In the Howard murder case, in McDuffie, Col. Tutt was thought to have made a better speech than General Gartrell, of Atlanta. In the Akin Stanford case, McDuffie County, Col. Tutt was pitted against Judge Twiggs, and lost nothing by comparison. The trial was full of dramatic incident, and while Stanford "came clear," public sentiment was with Col. Tutt.

"In a very desperate case in Columbia County, Col. Tutt was appointed by the court to defend two prisoners. The Colonel asked to be allowed to confer with his clients. Request granted, of course. The Colonel and his clients were conducted to one of the lower rooms of the court-house, and were left alone. After awhile, the court thought the conference between the Colonel and his clients had lasted long enough. They were sent for. The Colonel was found, but his clients weren't. They were gone. They were climbing the Appling hills, and making for the creek swamps. They were not in sight, and have never been seen in Columbia County since. The uproar in court was tremendous. Judge Pottle bellowed with wrath. The bar seethed with excitement. Everybody talked at once, and nobody knew what to do about it. Judge Pottle fussed and fumed and puffed and blowed; but the upshot was that *nothing* was done. The Colonel afterwards defended his conduct by saying that the court had appointed him to do his best for the prisoners, and the best he could do was to tell them to run. He undoubtedly saved their necks. [Note; Judge Joseph Pottle later became a private attorney and served as co-counsel with Col. Tutt on Elvira's seduction case against Sol. Jones.]

"Col. Tutt was the most brilliant member of the Gubernatorial Convention of 1884. He made a speech against the Two-thirds rule that killed it. The gist of his argument lay in the words, "I never could see why it required more votes to nominate a candidate than it does to elect him!" Standing in the gallery of the old James Opera House, and looking down upon the convention, I was a witness to Col. Tutt's magnificent triumph. An old fellow, of large physical proportions, arose while Col. Tutt was speaking, and asked – "But what do you think is due to a respectable minority?" Like a flash, Col. Tutt answered blandly – "I think it is the duty of *a respectable* minority, to bow to the will of the majority." The convention broke into a storm of laughter and applause, and the old man shut up, and collapsed. It was in this speech that the Colonel referred to himself as "Plain Bill Tutt," a name that lingered a long while. Afterwards, Tutt rose to speak a second time, but did not immediately gain recognition from the Chairman. Henry Grady, sitting at the front, saw what Tutt was intending, and he dashed off a note, in these words – 'Dear Bill, a *good* thing is the easiest thing to spoil: don't speak any more.   H. W. G.' A page ran with the note: Tutt read it, looked quickly at Grady, smiled acquiescence, and sat down. For months afterwards, Plain Bill Tutt was the name that was oftenest on men's lips. I have thought that if Colonel Tutt had *then* taken fortune at the flood, he might have risen high in the national councils.

"But, I must hurry on, and bring this sketch to a close.

"Col. Tutt was the wheel-horse of the Stephens campaign of 1882, his stump speeches being classed with those of Ranse Wright. He was the most powerful debater in the State Senate, where he met such combatants as Flem du Bignon, Tom Oliver and Milton Reese. He bore the brunt of Seab Reese's fight for Congress, and was, more than any one man, the cause of Reese's nomination. It did not seem to occur to Col. Tutt that he was a greater favorite for the place than was Seab himself. Thus, he allowed the golden period to pass, and it never comes but once. But, most of us make the same mistake, in one way or another.

"Col. Tutt grew dissatisfied with Thomson, and moved away, first to Augusta, and then to Elberton. 'The oak at forty cannot be transplanted;' and the man who tries to make a new home in the afternoon of life does not often succeed. The Colonel never reappeared in our courts after his removal to Augusta. He probably never made the deep impression in Elbert that he had made in McDuffie.

"Looking back, now, upon the years that have gone, I can see his fine manly qualities more distinctly than when we were eager rivals at the bar. The old passions have all died away. The remembrance of jealousies serve but to feed regrets. The W. D. Tutt who put on the grey jacket when a mere stripling, and who followed the Stars and Bars of the Southern Confederacy for four years, should not be forgotten. The W. D. Tutt who was an honest man, a brilliant orator, a true democrat, a loyal friend, and a foe who fought fair, should not be forgotten. The W. D. Tutt who was always proud of Lincoln County, and whose failing footsteps took him back to his old home to die among the people whom he knew best and loved best, should not be forgotten.

"Long is the roll of Lincoln County's honored sons, men who have represented her worthily in every profession, on almost every field of human effort; and that Roll of Honor will not be complete without the name of '*PLAIN BILL TUTT*.'"

****

Exhibit (2) Birth Date of Elvira Ivey

The date of Elvira Ivey's birth is somewhat questionable. Records indicate several different dates, but the date that seems most consistent with known facts is December 20, 1863. The 1870 Census states that she was 8 years old, which would indicate she was born in 1861, as the census was taken in August. The 1880 Census does not seem to have a record of Elvira; some families were missed altogether when the census was taken. The 1890 Census was destroyed by fire in Washington, D.C.; in the 1900 Census, Elvira was noted with a birth year of 1865; the 1910 Census indicated a birth year of 1863; and her tombstone recorded 1866 as her year of birth. The newspaper accounts surrounding her arrest and trial would indicate a birth year of 1863 or so; and finally, her "troubles" started about 7 years before her arrest, and it is reasonable to assume this was around the time of her "coming of age," which, in the 1800s was about age 14. The exact year of Elvira's birth is an educated guess at best, with all these conflicting records.

Exhibit (3) Disparity - Males and Females

Data from the 1870 census was quoted in The *Atlanta Weekly Sun,* 15 April, 1873: "...it will be perceived that the female over the male population predominates in the Southern states. The excess of females in the South may be attributable to the great loss of males in the late war, which has not been made up by European emigration. Georgia has an excess of 26,199 females."

Exhibit (4) Lore from the Extended Ivey Family

Several members of the extended Ivey family were willing to share their recollections concerning the story of Elvira. One family member noted that their elders did not speak too much about the story, but did share some information. Generally, the feeling of the family was that Elvira did *not* kill Jack McCauley, and she was covering for another family member, possibly her brother or father. They also spoke of how pretty Elvira was, and it was mentioned that Tom Watson said she would *not* be convicted. The previous discussion concerning Elvira's time in the Jefferson County jail was shared as well.

A member of the Ivey family shared that years later after the death of John (Elvira's brother), there was an estate sale, and that the double-barrel shotgun belonging to John was sold. Supposedly Fannie Huff Ivey, John's widow, who was known to be a mean woman, stated something to the effect that "that gun has killed one man; it can surely kill another." This apparently was somewhat of a 'selling feature' of the weapon.

But perhaps the most interesting bit of family lore is that it was said that John Marion Ivey, (Elvira's brother who some thought actually pulled the trigger) had a most notable habit for his life after the murder; he would frequently stop at the end of rows while plowing, and fall down on his knees and pray. There was some presumption by the family that this behavior may have been due to his feelings of guilt surrounding the murder. Perhaps related to this, is the fact that he wished to be buried in the Reedy Creek Baptist Church cemetery (his church), but his wife would not allow it; instead, he is buried in a somewhat overgrown cemetery on the old family farm where the murder occurred.

Exhibit (5) The Description of Elvira Ivey in the Press:

This represents a collection of terms and phrases used to describe Elvira:

Paramour; adventuress; desperado; prosecutrix; plucky woman; an unfortunate family; pretty murderess; pleasant face; converses cheerfully; displays no evidence of fear or anxiety; prisoner; fair slayer; young lady; quite attractive in person, but uneducated and illiterate; woman of great coolness and decision; beautiful young woman of 21 summers; brown hair and eyes; fair complexion; weighs 140 pounds; at one time a leader in Jefferson society; not the guilty person; object of great interest, being a woman of decided beauty; an attractive an appearance as is ever shown by a criminal at the bar; handsome and pretty face, youthful; "the only marked features of her face are, a large chin and a bold, prominent eye. She was prettily dressed in a dress trimmed with delicate crimson and on her head she wore a light straw hat crowned with a crimsoned plume"; pregnant condition; defendant; poor, unfortunate woman; friendless and forlorn captive; debauched, dishonored, but still dearly loved daughter;…when her daughter [Elvira] was pure and spotless; unfortunate darling; cheeks showed the bleaching of her long confinement in jail; quite a handsome girl; dressed in good taste; moved about the court room with a grace suited to a drawing room; fascinating young woman; prisoner; and firm person.

Exhibit (6) List of Lawyers for Elvira's Court Cases:

W. D. Tutt

Fred Tutt Lockhart

R. L. Gamble Jr.

Hurst Edward Hunter

James Granberry Cain

J. W. Polhill

Joseph Pottle

Wm. M. Howard

J. C. C. Black

Exhibit (7) News Sources – Elvira Ivey

16 December, 1884; The *Savannah Morning News*:

"A MYSTERIOUS MURDER.

CAMAK, GA., Dec. 15. – John McCauley, a resident of this county, was murdered last Friday night at the house of a Mr. Ivey, about 8 miles from Warrenton, near the line of Warren and Glascock counties. He is supposed to have gone there to visit Miss Elvira Ivey, who was stopping at the house in question with her brother. It is said that McCauley had about $1,500 in money with him, which was found on the ground under his body in an envelope. It is not thought that he was killed for the money. It is said that Miss Ivey swore at the inquest that she did the shooting, which is not believed. McCauley has a wife living, who left him about a month ago on account of Miss Ivey, who, it is said, has disappeared."

17 December, 1884; The *Warrenton Clipper*:

"A WOMAN'S FATAL SHOT.

A Deserting Husband Meets his Death at the Hands of his Paramour."

"Near a place called Reedy Creek church in Jefferson county, on inst. Saturday morning at about two o'clock, was the scene of a dark and bloody murder. Mr. A. J. McCauley, a well known citizen of Warren county, residing in the neighborhood of Brier Creek church, was the victim. The air is thick with rumors as to how and by whom he came to his death and whole affair seems to be shrouded in an impenetrable veil of mystery.

"Learning that Mrs. McCauley, the wife of the deceased, was stopping with friends in Warrenton on Monday, we called to see her thinking perhaps that she could give us the most authentic account of the bloody deed. She had just left for her home before we arrived but the family kindly repeated to us what their visitor had said to them on the subject. It seems that the deceased and his wife had not lived happily together for the last two years. The estrangement was due to the fact that the husband was conducting a criminal intimacy with a young and unmarried white woman by the name of Ivey who resided a few miles distant. These illicit relations occasioned many eruptions in the home circle only to be succeeded by the calms incident to the predominance of conscience over passion. But about two weeks ago, the storm bursted forth with increased fury and a separation of the husband and the wife insued. Mr. McCauley, it is said had been very successful in his business operations and had accumulated a nice little property consisting of land, live stock and money. The latter was on deposit in a bank at Augusta. Shortly after the separation he is reported to have visited

Augusta and drawn from the bank about two thousand dollars. On last Friday afternoon, Mrs. McCauley states, her husband rode over into Jefferson to see Miss Ivey who was at the time visiting relatives in the county. The visit, she says, was in response to a letter from the woman telling him that she would leave the country with him if he would go for her. It is said that she was to meet him at a certain window of the house at which she was stopping, the location of the same being described in the letter. He appeared at the window as agreed upon and was met by the woman who threw a pair of shoes out to him, presumably preparatory for the previously arranged flight. She next threw out a box containing some articles of wearing apparel, which McCauley stooped to pick up when he received a heavy charge of buck shot in the mouth from a gun aimed in the window. We failed to learn the name of the party who discovered the victim of the tragedy, but all of the two thousand dollars which he is said to have had in his possession, was found on his person except about four hundred and ten dollars, which is missing.

"At the Coroner's inquest Miss Ivey testified we learn, that the deceased was shot by herself stating as her reason for doing the deed, that McCauley had threatened to kill her if she refused to go with him. She shortly afterward mysteriously disappeared and a search by the friends of the deceased failed to develop her whereabouts. There are many other circumstances connected with the tragedy that give to it a greater air of mystery but our space is limited and we forbear. A great deal of excitement prevails and it cannot at present be surmised what new coloring the affair will assume."

****

27 December, 1884; The *Americus Recorder* (Americus, Ga.):

"**TO BE TRIED.**

"**Elvira Ivey Surrenders and Will be Tried for Murder.**

"**LOUISVILLE, GA.,** Dec. 24. – The case of the State vs. Elvira Ivey is set for preliminary trial at Pope Hill in Jefferson county for Thursday, the first day of January. She is charged with murder, and the circumstances of her killing Jack McCauley, the man who came to her window one night last week with the threat of death unless she eloped with him, have been published.

"Elvira Ivey has surrendered and will go to trial. She has retained Messrs. Tutt and Lockhart of Augusta to defend her. Hon. W. D. Tutt now represents her in a case of seduction in which she is the prosecutrix, and it is thought by some that McCauley was attempting to get her out of the way on the eve of the trial, when he met his death at the hands of the plucky woman and from the buck-shot of his own gun."

****

13 January, 1885; The *Mercury* (Sandersville, Ga.):

"Col. O. H. Rogers was regularly inducted in to office, as Solicitor General, at Louisville on Dec. 22nd." [O. H. Rogers was the law partner of J. K. Hines.]

****

11 Feb., 1885: The *Savannah Morning News*:

"Miss Vira Ivey, the Jefferson county woman desperado, was arrested by George Kelley, Sheriff of Jefferson county, Saturday and lodged in jail. On the night of Dec. 12, 1884, Jack McCauley appeared at her room window to run away with her, and was taking her goods as she handed them out to him, when, upon looking up again he received a charge of buckshot in the head. She was at the inquest and swore that she did the killing, but gave the officers the dodge and left or concealed herself. Her uncle (Tom Ivey), an ex-convict, has been making arrangements for the past two weeks to deliver her to the authorities in secret and save her commitment trial, with the view of employing good counsel and clearing her; but, fortunately, enough knew it to post the Sheriff on the road, who gathered her in before she reached the court house, and conveyed her behind the bars. Her Uncle Tom was also arrested by the Sheriff of McDuffie county, who had several warrants against him for forgery, perjury and carrying concealed weapons, etc."

****

19 Feb., 1885; The *Macon Telegraph* (Macon, Ga.):

"AN UNFORTUNATE FAMILY.

"Last week Sheriff Speir arrested and lodged in jail at this place Mr. Thomas J. Ivey, against whom there are three indictments in McDuffie Superior Court, charging him with perjury, cheating and swindling. It is charged that he drew his pay as a witness in said court, claiming to be a resident of Jefferson, while in fact he lived at the time in Warren county. Mr. Ivey protests his innocence and asserts that he can establish it. The arrest was made at Pope Hill in Jefferson county, where Mr. Ivey had gone to attend the preliminary trial of his niece, Miss Elvira Ivey, for the murder of Jack McCauley. – *Thomson Journal*."

****

20 Feb., 1885; The *Macon Weekly Telegraph*:

"Louisville's Female Murderess.

"….Miss Ivey…has a pleasant face, converses cheerfully, and displays no evidence of fear or anxiety….. *Louisville News*."

****

21 Feb., 1885; The *Macon Telegraph*:

"Tuesday, the 17th the commitment trial of Miss Elvira Ivey, of Warren county, …was heard at the court house in this place before J. W. White, notary public. The house was full of people from far and near…..

"Mr. Abel Russell was sworn for the State and testified that ….Miss Ivey confessed at the inquest….that she heard him [McCauley] take hold of the window shutter, and she stepped back and got a double-barrel shot gun, cocked it, laid it on the window and shot without taking any aim; she said she shot him in self-defense. Mr. Russell also said that the window is about six and a half feet from the ground. He saw the dead man about 10 o'clock on Saturday; was lying on the ground near the window….

"…W. S. Thompson, being sworn, said that the package of letters were found locked up in the house of the deceased, that he saw the deceased's wife get them out of a drawer….

"The court then committed the prisoner to jail for manslaughter, and set the bond for release at $1,500. *Savannah News*."

****

22 Feb., 1885; The *Columbus Daily Enquirer-Sun* (Columbus, Ga.):

"Miss Elvira Ivey, who shot and killed A. J. McCauley, of Warren county, in Augusta last week under mysterious circumstances, has been bound over to appear before the superior court to be tried for manslaughter. The case is an interesting and mysterious one, and will be a celebrated one in the court annals of the state."

****

24 Feb., 1885; The *Weekly Constitution* (Atlanta, Ga.):

"LOUISVILLE, GA., February 17. – [Special.]– Miss S. E. Ivey, the slayer of J. C. McCauley, has to-day in justice court, been tried and committed for manslaughter. She will doubtless give bond. The prosecution was argued in a forcible and masterly manner by Attorney Colley, and Messrs. Tutt and Gamble came forward in an able and eloquent defense. The case is a very strong one; the lawyers, and indeed others, declaring that they had never read or heard tell of another similar one."

****

27 Feb., 1885; The *True Citizen* (Waynesboro, Ga.):

"MYSTERIOUS MURDER.

"The Preliminary Hearing of a Remarkable Case.

"Augusta Chronicle.

"No killing in Georgia has excited more comment and discussion than the shooting of A. J. McCauley, of Warren county; by Miss Elvira Ivey. The circumstances of the killing are entirely unknown save as detailed by Miss Ivey herself. She is a young lady about twenty-two years old, quite attractive in person, but uneducated and illiterate. She is a woman of great coolness and decision and admits the killing of McCauley, and claims that she was justified in doing so. She was on a visit to her brother John Ivey, in Jefferson county.

"Her statement before the coroner's jury is the only testimony as to the killing. She says she was awakened about 2 o'clock by some one knocking on her window. She went to the window whereupon it was jerked open by a man standing upon the ground beneath it, who said: 'I will give you $1,500 to go with me.' She did not know who the man was, but thought it was McCauley. She drew back and he said: 'If you don't hand your things out the window and come ahead I'll blow your brains out.' She immediately handed out her shoes and a paper box sitting near, and then as if getting something else to hand him reached a gun setting near by and thrusting it out the window fired into the man's face. She then knocked at her brother's door and told him she had killed a man at her window whom she thought was McCauley, though she was not certain. McCauley, when examined by the neighbors, who were summoned next morning, had $1,590 in his pocket book, and had a pocket knife open in his right hand breeches pocket. The load entered one side of his mouth, and ranged down through his neck and shoulder. These were the circumstances of the killing as detailed by the sole witness to the tragedy.

"Now, in order to understand the theory of the prosecution and the defense in the case, it is necessary to know that there is another case in Warren county in which Miss Elvira Ivey is prosecuting Sol Jones for seduction. Many attempts had been made to settle the case by defendant without avail.

"The killing of McCauley occurred on Saturday night, and the trial of Sol Jones was set for the Monday following. Miss Ivey says she had heard threats made against her life, and everything was done to stop the trial and prejudice the people against her. Having heard these threats, she was in fear of her life, and killed the man at her window under the belief that his mission was to carry into effect the threats she had heard.

"On the contrary, the State introduced about a score of letters purporting to have been written by Miss Ivey to McCauley. These letters are most endearing in their terms and damaging to Miss Ivey's reputation. None of them are dated or addressed to anyone, and only one is signed. The one is signed Elvira Ivey and signed twice, one being in different ink. These letters are claimed to embrace about a year, and one of them, it is claimed, refers to the night of the killing. This letter makes an appointment for McCauley to come to the window and elope with her. It is claimed that this was only a device to get him to the window and kill him; that he went there in accordance with the appointment made in the note and was killed. The State, however, fails to introduce any motive whatever that Miss Ivey had for wanting to kill him, and the language of the note indicates warmest love for McCauley.

"Miss Ivey claims that she was only casually acquainted with McCauley; that she never wrote to him in her life, and was never in his company but a few times. She says Sol Jones was trying to get her out of the way to prevent a trial of the case against him, and McCauley, as his friend, was induced to make way with her by abduction, murder, or in some way. She says the letters are forgeries, manufactured to injure her reputation and prejudice the public against her in the other trial. The letters, it is claimed, were found in a table drawer in McCauley's house, the key to which always hung on the mantle. The letters were identified as the writing of Miss Ivey by only one witness, James Norris, the uncle of Sol Jones. He claimed to be familiar with her handwriting from the fact that in 1879, while at a party, she had written him a note, stating that her horse had gotten loose, and asking him to carry her home. He had not seen any of her writing since. There are several inconsistencies in the case, and it is a mysterious killing. The prosecution claims that McCauley was there to run off with her by appointment, and yet he came on horseback with only one horse, and had an open knife in his pocket. It is further claimed that the promise to run off with him was made merely to get him where she could kill him. On the door of the house in which she was visiting, on the fences and on the houses, lewd pictures and obscene pictures and writings were posted, and Miss Ivey says threats were made against her life. She supposed the man at the window was Sol Jones' emissary, who was set to get her out of the way, and she killed him to protect herself.

"A few days ago a sensational article was published claiming that Miss Ivey had assumed the killing of McCauley to shield her brother who, in reality, had done the shooting. This Miss Ivey emphatically denies, and says her brother knew nothing of it until she told him after it was over; that she killed McCauley herself; that she believes she was justified in doing it, and under the same circumstances would do so again.

"A preliminary hearing was had before Justice White, of Louisville, and she was bound over to the Superior Court under the charge of manslaughter. The prosecution is represented by F. H. Colley, Esq., of Washington, and Messrs. Phillips and Wrenn, of Louisville, and Tutt and Lockhart, of Augusta, represent Miss Ivey. The case is an interesting and mysterious one and will be a celebrated one in the court annals of the State."

****

13 March, 1885; The *Augusta Chronicle*;

"THE JACK MCCAULEY KILLING.

Editors Chronicle:

"THOMSON, GA., March 12. – Some time ago you published a communication in which were set forth the contending theories as to the killing of Jack McCauley. Your correspondent states among other things that Elvira Ivey is prosecuting Sol Jones for seduction in Warren Superior Court, and that her defense for the killing was based upon the idea that Jack McCauley was acting as Jones' friend in an attempt to abduct her.

"The one circumstance your correspondent mentions which gives any color to the 'abduction theory' is that McCauley was killed on Saturday night and that the trial of Sol. Jones was fixed for the following Monday.

"When I first noticed the article mentioned, I did not think any correction necessary, although I was asked to make one in behalf of Sol. Jones whom I defend in the seduction case, but I find that the statement alluded to, passing without denial and therefore taken as true, tends to prejudice the case of my client, and I therefore ask space to correct it.

"Your correspondent is mistaken when he says that the trial of Jones was to have taken place the Monday following the killing of McCauley on Saturday night. The seduction case is in Warren Superior Court; no other court can try him unless it be impossible to get a jury in that county. The regular terms of the court are held in October and in April. The October term had been finally adjourned long before McCauley was killed, and no other session was to be had until its regular meeting in April, 1885. There was a County Court at Warrenton on the Monday following the killing of McCauley, but Jones' case was not there and could not have been there because the County Court has no jurisdiction to try a seduction case.

"So far from McCauley having been such a friend to Jones that he was ready to assume in his behalf the dangerous task of an abductor, they were not on speaking terms. What caused this enmity can be readily supposed. Again, McCauley had repeatedly expressed his entire sympathy with the prosecution of Jones, and had expressed his willingness to aid that prosecution, if necessary, with his money. Finally, your correspondent rather intimates that it is strange that McCauley alone should come with one horse to elope with Miss Ivey. If it is strange that one man with one horse should attempt an elopement, the girl being willing, is it not stranger that he should attempt an abduction, the girl being unwilling?

"I have no desire to enter further into the facts than is necessary in simple defense of my client. He is soon, like Miss Ivey, to be tried for a very grave offence. As I do not wish his case prejudiced, so I say nothing with intent to prejudge hers. And if your correspondent's purpose was to give a fair statement of both sides (and I presume that such was his purpose) he will receive this correction is the same spirit that prompts it. Yours truly, THOS. E. WATSON."

****

18 April, 1885; The *Savannah Morning News*:

"…The case of the State vs. Elvira Ivey, charged with the murder of McCauley, will also come up at this term, and no doubt take up considerable time and money in the way of trials, continuances, etc."

****

14 May, 1885; The *Columbus Daily Enquirer-Sun* (Columbus, Ga.):

"An interesting case is docketed in Jefferson county for the superior court now in session. It is that of the state against Saucel Elvira Ivey, who stands charged with the murder of Jack McCauley, in Jefferson county, on the night of the 12th of December, 1884. Miss Ivey is a beautiful young woman of twenty-one summers, brown hair and eyes and fair complexion. She weighs 140 pounds. Public sentiment seems to be with her. It is thought she will be acquitted if the case comes to trial."

****

15 May, 1885; The *Sandersville Herald*:

"Solicitor-General O. H. Rogers is unable to attend Superior Court in Jefferson County this week; in consequence of a painful rising on his face. Mr. W. L. Phillips we see is acting in his stead this week."

****

15 May, 1885; The *New York Times*:

"A SINGULAR MURDER CASE.

A YOUNG WOMAN CONFESSES THE CRIME TO SAVE ANOTHER.

"LOUISVILLE, Ga., May 14. – The Superior Court of Jefferson County is at present engaged in the trial of a sensational murder case, in which a young woman is standing at the bar of justice. Miss Elvira Ivey was at one time a leader in Jefferson society, but an indiscretion closed the doors of many people against her. A suit was pending against Solomon Jones, the object of which was to compel him to restore Miss Ivey's good name by marriage. This suit was to be called in court on Monday morning. On the Sunday morning preceding, however, the community was thrown into intense excitement by the news that the dead body of Mr. John McCauley, one of the wealthiest farmers of Warren, had been found under the window of Miss Ivey's room. A bullet had pierced his temple. In his left hand was clutched a bunch of bank bills, amounting to $1,500.

"When Miss Ivey told the story of the dead man's presence there excitement was greatly increased. She alleged that McCauley was a friend of Jones, and that the object of his visit was to induce her to withdraw her claims against his friend. As a means to accomplish this he protested his own love for her, showed her the roll of bills, and urged her to fly to Texas with him. As McCauley had a living wife and seven small children Miss Ivey reminded him of his duty toward them. With an oath the desperate man declared that he intended that Miss Ivey should either elope with him or suffer death, at the same time making a motion to enter the window. Instantly the bullet from Miss Ivey's pistol compelled him to release his hold from the window, and he fell back dead. To her father and brother, who were brought to the spot by the pistol's report, she told the story, and declared that the whole movement was a plot to save Jones in the approaching trial.

"The discovery of a package of letters, however, in the possession of McCauley did not accord with the girl's statements. In these letters, covering over a year preceding the killing, and contemporaneous with her intimacy with Jones, she writes in the most endearing manner to McCauley. All the terms in use among lovers are used, and coming from a single girl to a man whom she knew to be married they are very damaging. In one of these letters, supposed to be the last, though not dated, assent is given to the proposition to elope to Texas, and the night upon which the killing took place is designated as the time. Why, then, did Miss Ivey kill him instead of flying with him? This is the mystery. Her letters establish her intimacy with him. That he was not on speaking terms with Jones, owing to their rivalry, was well known. The only explanation which has been widely published through the State, is that McCauley was an expected caller at the window that night; that the noise the couple in removing articles through the window awakened a third party, who, seeing a man in an improper place, fired, killing him; and that seeing the mischief done Miss Ivey assumed the crime as a shield for this third party. Ever since the crime was committed the community has been stirred up with sensational reports, in which names have been variously used, but one thing seems to be certain, that Miss Ivey will not be convicted. So strong is the belief that she is not the guilty person that is it not believed the jury will leave the box, but will acquit her at once. Miss Ivey, as she sits in the court room, is an object of great interest, being a woman of decided beauty."

****

15 May, 1885; The *True Citizen* (Waynesboro, Ga.):

"Miss Ivey on Trial.

Atlanta Constitution.

"SUMMERVILLE, GA., May 12. – Jefferson superior court convened yesterday. Judge Carswell delivered an able charge to the grand jury, which organized with George F. Hudson as foreman. Solicitor-General Rogers is absent on account of sickness and Mr. Phillips is acting in his stead.

"The most important case for trial at this term of court is that of state against Saucel Elvira Ivey, who stands charged with the murder of Jack McCauley, in this county, on the night of the 12th of December, 1884. Miss Ivey is a beautiful young woman of twenty-one summers, brown hair and eyes and fair complexion. She weighs 140 pounds. Public sentiment here seems to be with her. It is thought she will be acquitted if the case comes to trial. Messrs. Tutt, Hunter & Gamble are her lawyers."

****

16 May, 1885; *Courrier des Etats-Unis* (New York, N. Y.);

[Newspaper in French carried article about one-half of a column on case.]

****

17 May, 1885; The *Savannah Morning News*:

"ELVIRA IVEY CONVICTED.

"5 YEARS IMPRISONMENT THE SENTENCE OF THE COURT.

"Hundreds of People in Attendance on the Trial - A Motion for a New Trial Already Filed – The Story of the Woman's Indiscreet Amours and the Fatal Shot.

"LOUISVILLE, GA., May 16. – In the case of the State against Elvira Ivey, charged with the murder of A. J. McCauley on Dec. 12, 1884, the defendant was today convicted of voluntary manslaughter and sentenced to five years imprisonment in the penitentiary. The counsel for the defendant have filed a motion for a new trial. The court room has been crowded since last Thursday. It was estimated that 500 persons were present last night in the court room. The counsel for the prosecution took up a great deal of time trying to get some letters admitted in evidence said to have been written by the defendant to McCauley. The letters were admitted.

"THE FATAL SHOT…." [Balance of article already included in other sources]

****

20 May, 1885; The *Augusta Chronicle*:

"ELVIRA IVEY.

The Trial, the Evidence, the Counsel and the Result.

Correspondent of the Chronicle.

"**LOUISVILLE, GA**., May 18. - One of the most important cases that has been tried in the section of Georgia is that of the State vs. Elvira Ivey, charged with the murder of Jack McCauley...

...The State rebutted her statement by showing at the inquest In that confession she stated that between the hours of 2 and 3 o'clock in the morning of December 13th, she heard a knocking at the window of a small room adjoining hers. She went to it to peep out and see who it was. About the time she reached it some one jerked open the window and said, "Come and go with me and I will give you fifteen hundred dollars." She was frightened and shrank back, when the same voice said: "If you don't hand out your things and come with me, I will blow your brains out." Pretending to comply with his order, she handed out a paper box and a pair of shoes, until she could get back to a gun in the corner of the room. Reaching it she came forward, laid it upon the window sill and fired. She then went into an adjoining room and told her brother that she had killed a man at her window.

"In her statement to the jury, she said her troubles commenced when she began to prosecute Sol. Jones of Warren county, for seduction several years before. It was then the parties began posting vulgar and obscene placards about her all over the county – at churches and at her father's door – filled with threats against her if she did not abandon the prosecution of Jones. She left Warren county and went to Jefferson to visit her brother. They followed her down there and continued to post like notices all over that neighborhood and at her brother's door, and they had even followed her to the jail here, a letter having been dropped at the jail door last Saturday night threatening her with death before she could get home if the jury acquitted her. She said she opened the window, and also proved by Jones that none of these letters were written to or received by him, and that he was not on speaking terms with McCauley at his death. McCauley was found lying on the ground under the window with $1,500 lying under him and about his person, and an open knife in his pocket. A pair of shoes and a paper box were also found on the ground…

…I cannot close without returning thanks to Col. Geo. Warren for the hospitable entertainment extended to your correspondent during the week.

J. J. G."

****

21 May, 1885; The *Savannah Morning News*:

"TRIAL OF ELVIRA IVEY.

The Facts of the Celebrated Case as They Were Developed at the Trial.

"**LOUISVILLE, GA**., May 18. – The case of the State vs. Elvira Ivey, charged with the murder of A. J. McCauley, which was tried in the Superior Court last week, attracted wide attention. In the papers of the State the facts were not generally correctly stated. One correspondent stated 'that Miss Ivey was at one time a leader in Jefferson society, but that an indiscretion closed the doors of the people against her.' This is a mistake. Miss Ivey was not known in Jefferson county until after the fatal shot. Miss Ivey's home was within about eight miles of Warrenton, in Warren county, and she had come to Jefferson to live with her brother only a few months before she committed the crime for which she was convicted. The weapon with which McCauley was killed was a double-barrel shotgun.

"The following is a brief and correct statement of the case: It appears from the evidence that A. J. McCauley was a married man, and had separated from his wife and was living alone on his farm in Warren county. The morning after McCauley was killed his wife came back to his house, and in looking over his things she came across a package of letters, numbering about forty or forty-five, in a table drawer. Among them was one signed "S. E. Ivey." This same letter Mrs. McCauley recollected seeing once before she separated from her husband. These letters were brought into court and offered in evidence. Counsel for defendant objected to their introduction, because the letters were not addressed to any one nor signed by any one. The State then introduced James Norris, of McDuffie county, who swore that he was acquainted with Miss Ivey's handwriting, from having received a short note from her at a party in 1879, asking him to carry her home. Also, that he had seen her write a song ballad and had seen some other writing of Miss Ivey's. Upon this showing, the court admitted about ten of the letters in evidence. The defendant's counsel made a strong fight to keep them out. Mr. Norris' manner of testifying was subject to criticism. A negro man by the name of Gus Hobbs testified that on Friday, Dec. 5, 1884, he met McCauley in Warrenton, and McCauley asked him to carry a letter for him to Miss Elvira Ivey, down in Jefferson county. Witness carried the letter and delivered it to Miss Ivey, as instructed, with the injunction not to let anyone see it but her. Miss Ivey gave him an answer, which he took back to McCauley. This is supposed to be the letter Miss Ivey sent by Hobbs in answer:

"'Mr._____: I have nothing to write that would interest you. I have not time to write much to you. I will go with you if you will come Friday after the first Sunday. Come below the house in that pine thicket, and I will see you after dark. Come to the window and I will give you my clothes. I will look for you. I think you have told falsehoods enough on me to send your soul to hell. I am sorry you and your wife have parted. If you can't live with her I am afraid you won't live with me. When we leave we will never come back here no more. Get you a home before you come after me. Good-bye. Be sure to come; be particular.'

"The State's counsel laid great stress on the above letter. He took the ground that McCauley was decoyed and persuaded to come to her house, that Miss Ivey might kill him; that she named the place and window to come to and the time. She told him in the letter to come on Friday after the first Sunday. This letter was not dated, but McCauley went there on Friday night after the first Sunday in December, 1884, and was shot while at the window. Miss Ivey's statement was about as follows:

"'My troubles commenced about six or seven years ago. I was seduced by Sol. Jones. I am now prosecuting him for seduction. I then lived with my father, Adam Ivey, in Warren county. My enemies were friends of Sol. Jones, and did all in their power to make me leave home by putting up placards on trees and churches and other places. I acknowledge writing some of the letters (meaning the letters in court), but did not write them to A. J. McCauley. I wrote them to Sol. Jones when I was engaged to him. I never wrote McCauley a letter in my life. I was in my room and heard some one at the window. I got up and went to the window. Somebody snatched the window open and insisted on my going with him. I refused to go. He said: "If you will go with me I will give you $1,500." I still refused. He then said: "I will shoot your brains out if you don't go." I then stepped back and handed him a paper box with some things. I then picked up the gun and shot out the window. I took no aim. I did not know it was McCauley until I was informed by somebody some time after. On McCauley's person was found $1,500 and a pocket knife opened in his pocket.

"Sol. Jones testified that the letters introduced were not written to him and that he had destroyed all letters written by Miss Ivey to him. He said he had not spoken to McCauley in about three years. There is now pending a prosecution in Warren Superior Court against Jones for the seduction of Miss Ivey. The defense claimed that McCauley was trying to abduct Miss Ivey in the interest of Sol. Jones and get her out of the way to keep her from appearing as a witness against Jones in the prosecution for seduction. The State was ably represented by W. L. Phillips, Solicitor General pro tem., and Hon. Thomas E. Watson, of McDuffie. Mr. Watson's argument to the jury was a masterpiece of ingenuity and eloquence.

"The defendant was represented by Messrs. Cain & Polhill, Gamble & Hauten, of Louisville, and W. D. Tull, of Augusta. R. L. Gamble, Jr., who for four years has so ably represented this circuit as Solicitor General, made the opening argument to the jury and presented his side of the case with force and ability. W. D. Tull made the closing argument, speaking about three hours. He made an earnest appeal too in behalf of Miss Ivey. Judge Carswell's charge was clear and forcible. The jury was out about five hours, and returned a verdict of voluntary manslaughter. The defendant was then sentenced to five years imprisonment in the penitentiary. A motion for a new trial was made. The verdict gives general satisfaction throughout the county."

****

21 May, 1885; The *Sandersville Herald*:

"Miss Elvira Ivey charged with the murder of Jack McCauley was found guilty of voluntary manslaughter at her trial in the Jefferson Superior Court last week. Miss Ivey in her statement, confessed that she did the shooting, but under fear that the murdered man would kill her.

"Letters from her to McCauley were admitted as evidence, produced by Mrs. McCauley, expressing her affection for him and readiness to elope with him although he was a married man.

"It is said many believe Miss Ivey did not do the shooting. She was sentenced to five years in the penitentiary. Motion was made for a new trial."

****

22 May, 1885; The *True Citizen* (Waynesboro, Ga.):

"The work of the superior courts in Jefferson and Richmond counties last week was very important. In the former Miss Ivey was tried for the murder of Jack McCauley, found guilty of voluntary manslaughter and sentenced to the penitentiary for the term of five years. This is one of the most mysterious cases that was ever tried in Georgia, and while she confessed to the killing, very grave doubts are entertained that she was the read perpetrator of the bloody deed. The public sympathy seemed to be in Miss Ivey's favor, and while McCauley's acts provoked him to be in pursuit of a most wicked deed, her correspondence with him showed that she was not guiltless. The verdict of the jury has been accepted by the public as a correct one. – She will, of course, apply for a new trial."

****

22 May, 1885; *Macon Weekly Telegraph*:

"A PRETTY MURDERESS.

A HIGHLY SENSATIONAL TRIAL AT LOUISVILLE, GA.

Elvira Ivey Convicted of Manslaughter in Killing Jackson McCauley – Circumstances Attending the Crime – The Sentence.

"… Among her acquaintances was Mr. Solomon Jones, a young farmer in the neighborhood, who took advantage of his engagement to her to seduce her. The result of this indiscretion was a demand on the part of Miss Ivey's father to restore her good name by a marriage. This Jones refused to do, and charges of seduction were preferred against him. To avoid any such result, Jones confided his troubles to an uncle named Norris, who in turn enlisted the aid and sympathies of A. Jackson McCauley, who is a young farmer. McCauley, it seems, was a married man, with two children, and how was in love with the fair Miss Ivey. The testimony develops the fact that a plan was made by Norris and McCauley to induce Miss Ivey to elope with him, and thus allow the suit against Jones to fall through for want of prosecution.

"…Such was the sympathy of the people for the unfortunate woman, that the sheriff, G. W. Kelly, a kind-hearted and very efficient officer, allowed her all the liberty of the jail consistent with security.

"…When the case was called on Thursday, people flocked from all parts of the country to the court house to get a glimpse of the fair slayer. Interest was at white heat during the entire progress of the trial, and the high character and ability of the array of counsel invested the case with considerable importance.

"…McCauley and wife lived in Warren county together for twelve years.

"…State introduced a witness who swore he carried a letter from McCauley to Miss Ivey a week before the killing. This Miss Ivey denied.

"The interest the case inspired was shown in the vast crowd of white and colored people that have been crowding the court room for the three days consumed in the trial, the case having been sounded out Thursday morning and submitted to the jury at noon to-day.

"Argument began last night at 8 o'clock, R. L. Gamble, Jr., for four years the able solicitor –general for this circuit, making the opening speech for the defense, on the line that the case was a conspiracy between Sol Jones and Norris to get rid of Miss Ivey's testimony in the case against Jones for seduction; that no letter had been written by her to McCauley agreeing to elope with him and that her statement as to the transaction was true, and that she killed him in self defense. The speech was an able one and increased the sympathy of the vast crowd for the fair prisoner. He was followed by Hon. T. E. Watson, of McDuffie, for the State, in an ingenious, logical and eloquent appeal to the jury. It was plainly seen that his argument had made its effect upon the spectators at least. It was said by the crowd that had Mr. Watson the closing speech the result would have been greatly feared by Miss Ivey's friends.

"Court then adjourned until 8 o'clock this morning, when Hon. W. D. Tutt, of Augusta, long celebrated as an able criminal lawyer, resumed the argument, making the closing speech, occupying fully two hours. His appeal to the jury was beautiful and touching, causing a pathetic scene in court.

"The hour of noon having arrived, the jury was charged by Judge Carswell and retired.

"Miss Ivey, whose cheeks showed the bleaching of her long confinement in jail, is quite a handsome girl, dressed in good taste, and moved about the court room with a grace suited to a drawing room. She was accompanied by her mother, and a portion of the time she held her little infant in her lap. The spectacle was a sad one. Such a scene is seldom witnessed in a Georgia court of justice."

****

26 May, 1885; The *Butler Herald* (Butler,Ga.):

"A WOMAN'S CRIME.

THE CHARGE AGAINST MISS ELVIRA IVEY.

LOUISVILLE, GA., May 15. -The case against Miss Elvira Ivey, charged with the manslaughter of Jack McCauley, cause intense interest here…

ELVIRA IVEY FOUND GUILTY.

"…As to the killing Miss Ivey claimed that it was done because her life was threatened. The State contended the it was premeditated, that the watch dogs were housed that they might not scare McCauley away from the window, that the gun was ready cocked, that the girl was expecting him and wanted him killed, because the room where the killing was done was not her room and she had no business there, that it was an empty room, and it was strange that the gun should be in that room.

"On her statement Miss Ivey admitted that some of the letters were genuine, but that they were written to Sol Jones. The prosecution claimed that if one of the letters were genuine they all were, and that they showed it, and furthermore that they contained statements which showed beyond all question that they were not written to Jones.

"The trial commenced Thursday after dinner, ran on all day Friday and into Friday night until 12 o'clock. Then on Saturday at 11 o'clock it was given to the jury, who, after being out five hours returned a verdict of guilty of manslaughter. Defendant was sentenced to five years in the penitentiary."

****

27 May, 1885; The *Abbeville Messenger* (Abbeville, S. C.):

"LOUISVILLE, May 16. - As McCauley had a living wife and seven children, Miss Ivey reminded him of his duty toward them. ...Since Thursday at noon, the court room has been crowded with spectators from Jefferson and contiguous Counties. Much of the time was taken up in argument on the admissibility of certain letters claimed by the prosecution to have been written by Miss Ivey to McCauley, expressing affection for him, and avowing her readiness to skip with him, though a married man. The letters were admitted as evidence, though containing no address or signature. Mrs. McCauley heavily veiled with the deepest black, testified as to said letters being in possession of her husband at the time of his death. ... Sol. Jones, who is now being prosecuted in Warren Superior Court for the alleged seduction of Miss Ivey, appeared as witness in court…..The jury were boarded at the Central Hotel during their session on the case, and it is said stood first, ten for acquittal and two for conviction. The sentence is for five years in the penitentiary.... *Columbia Register*."

****

4 June, 1885; The *Savannah Morning News*:

"Louisville correspondence NEWS, June 2: The motion for a new trial in the case of the State vs. Elvira Ivey was argued today in the Superior Court of Jefferson county. Judge Carswell granted Miss Ivey a new trial."

****

17 October, 1885; The Augusta Chronicle:

"THE ELVIRA IVEY CASE.

SOL. JONES DECLARED NOT GUILTY – POINTS ABOUT WARREN COUNTY.

"THOMSON, Ga., October 16. – [Special correspondence.] – Warren Superior Court convened last week, Judge Lumpkin presiding, and his manner of dispatching business is remarkable. A very heavy docket was on hand. The most important civil case was that of Louise Myrick vs. the Kinsley estate. The amount involved was $30,000. [illegible amount].

"The most important criminal case was that of the State vs. Sol. Jones, charged with the seduction of Miss Elvira Ivey, who has since become widely known as the alleged murderess of Jack McCauley. She was the State's main witness, and testified that Sol. Jones took advantage of an engagement existing between them to accomplish her ruin. She is a very handsome and fascinating young woman of about 25 years of age.

"The defense proposed to prove that Miss Ivey had been guilty of similar bad conduct before the alleged seduction. The Judge ruled out this testimony because the witnesses could not swear positively that this conduct was before the alleged seduction. The defense then impeached Elvira Ivey by two grand jurors who served in finding the indictment, and by proof of contradictory statements.

"The jury after being out ten or fifteen minutes returned with a verdict of not guilty. Counsel for prosecution were Messrs. Tutt, Pottle and Howard, for the defense, Messrs. Watson and Whitehead. Very fine and able arguments were made on both sides. H."

****

12 Nov., 1885; *Louisville News & Farmer*:

"SUPERIOR COURT.

"This court was convened in this place Monday morning, Judge Carswell presiding. ... Solicitor O. H. Rogers is in attendance looking after the criminal business of the court…Monday the case of the State against Elvira Ivey charged with the McCauley murder, was called and continued till the next term because of the sickness of Mrs. McCauley, the widow of the slain man…."

****

15 May, 1886; The *Savannah Morning News*:

"Jefferson Superior Court convened on May 12. Several minor cases have been disposed of. The case of the State vs. Miss Elvira Ivey for the murder of Jack McCauley was continued until the November term."

****

27 May, 1886; The *Sandersville Herald*:

"The case of the State vs. Miss Elvira Ivey of Jack McCauley came up in Jefferson court and was continued until November term."

****

17 May, 1887; The *Weekly Telegraph* (Macon, Ga.):

[Information about Fred Morgan case also in this article, along with others in the Jefferson Superior Court.]

"Miss Elvira Ivey, charged with murder, did not put in her appearance. Her bond was forfeited."

****

17 May, 1887; The *Atlanta Constitution*:

"Elvira Ivey, the Jefferson County murderess, through a fortunate attack of the measles, has secured another continuance of her case."

****

17 Nov., 1887; The *Louisville News & Farmer*:

"NOT GUILTY.

"Just as we go to press at dark, the jury in the Elvira Ivey case brought in a verdict of not guilty. And so the big murder case is settled at last."

****

20 November, 1887; The *Savannah Morning News*:

"At Louisville the Superior Court has been in session since Monday morning, His Honor Judge J. K. Hines on the bench. Thursday ended the second trial of Miss Elvira Ivey for the murder of A. J. McCauley in the fall of 1884, for which she was tried the following spring, found guilty and sentenced to five years in the penitentiary by the then Judge, R. W. Carswell. It was a very hard matter to secure a jury. Several panels were exhausted, but finally the requisite number was secured. The verdict of not guilty was received by the immense crowds, both inside and out of the court house, with great satisfaction and loud cheers. Indeed, two of the most enthusiastic were fined $5 each for being too loud in their demonstrations."

****

21 November, 1887; The *Sun* (New York, N. Y.):

"MISS IVEY ACQUITTED. She Shot a Man who Threatened to Kill Her if She Didn't Elope with Him.

"AUGUSTA, GA., Nov. 20. – The celebrated case of Miss Elvira Ivey, in Jefferson county, which has been tried three times, has ended at last in the liberation of the fair defendant. …. Among her acquaintances was Solomon Jones, who took advantage of his engagement to her to mislead her. The result of this was a demand on the part of the girl's father that Jones marry her. This Jones refused to do, and charges of seduction were preferred against him.

"Jones confided his troubles to an uncle named Norris, who in turn enlisted the aid of A. Jackson McCauley, a well-to-do young farmer. McCauley, it seems, was a married man with two children, and was in love himself with Miss Ivey, and they had been intimate. The testimony developed the fact that a plan was made by Norris and McCauley to induce Miss Ivey to elope with the latter, and thus allow the suit against Jones to fall through for want of prosecution.

"….Miss Ivey was arrested and placed under the surveillance of the Sheriff for two months. Such was the sympathy of the people for the unfortunate woman that the Sheriff allowed her all the liberty of the jail consistent with security.

"…From a large batch of letters put in evidence, secret meetings between McCauley and the girl and criminal relations were shown to have long existed.

"…Miss Ivey was found guilty [first trial] but, pending a motion on a new trial, was let out on bail, and the jury in the trial just ended found her not guilty of murder and set her free."

****

22 Nov., 1887; The *Weekly Telegraph* (Macon, Ga.):

"TRIAL OF MISS IVEY.

She is Acquitted Amid Shouts of Approval from Her Friends.

"LOUISVILLE, GA., November 18. – Superior Court has been in session here since Monday morning, his Honor Judge J. K. Hines on the bench. The second trial of Miss Elvira Ivey, for the murder of A. J. McCaully in the fall of 1884, for which she was tried the following spring, found guilty and sentenced to five years in the penitentiary by the then Judge R. W. Carswell. It was a very hard matter to secure a jury. Several panels were exhausted but finally the requisite number was secured.

"The verdict of not guilty was received by the immense crowds, both inside and out of the court house, with great satisfaction and loud cheers. Indeed, two of the most enthusiastic were fined $5 each for being too loud in their demonstrations. Court will probably continue for the balance of this week."

****

22 Nov., 1887; The *Evening Star* (Washington, D. C.):

"A GEORGIA GIRLS' SHOT.

THE DEAD BODY OF HER LOVER FOUND BELOW HER CHAMBER WINDOW.

"Miss Elvira Ivey, a beautiful young woman, has been acquitted at Louisville, Ga., of the murder of A. J. McCauley. She had been tried once before and convicted, but the feeling against hanging a woman was so strong that it was an easy matter to secure a new trial."

****

24 Nov., 1887; The *Louisville News & Farmer*

"Wednesday evening the court took up the Elvira Ivey case, and by dark eleven jurors were selected. Bailiffs were sent in the country to hunt up jurors, all in town and attending court being rejected as most of them had heard the case and expressed an opinion or else were not acceptable to either side. This case will consume all of today (Thursday)."

****

24 Nov., 1887; The *Louisville News & Farmer*:

"SUPERIOR COURT.

"Thursday was taken up trying the Elvira Ivey case. The letters which the State claimed passed between her and McAuley, and other evidence were ruled out by the court, and the trial thereby shortened. Strong speeches were made for the defense by J. W. Polhill and R. L. Gamble, Jr., and Solicitor General Rogers plead the cause of the State in an able manner. The jury was out a few minutes, and returned with a verdict of not guilty. There was a little demonstration when the decision was announced, and it cost two gentlemen five dollars each in the nature of fines. One of the men is an uncle of Miss Ivey, and lives in Warren county and the other one is a quiet citizens of Jefferson county.

"And thus ends the big case. At the first trial, it will be remembered, the prisoner was convicted of manslaughter, and sentenced to the penitentiary for five years. But a new trial was granted by Judge Carswell on technical points. It was the opinion of most people then and is now that Miss Ivey did not kill McAuley. But she stood firm to the last that she did the shooting, and said it was because he threatened to kill her if she did not go with him. If she did not, why should she say she did? There was no material evidence to convict her or any of her family of the crime, and if she did not shoot McAuley, all she had to do to come free, was to deny it; for it was only by her confessing the crime there was ever any chance to convict her. And so the natural conclusion is that she did shoot him, and believing firmly she was justifiable in doing so, she was willing to confess it and stand a trail being confident of coming out clear. It must be admitted that she proved herself a firm person, for whether she killed the man or not, if she had denied it, or afterwards said her confession was false, she would have come clear without any trouble. Two of her attorneys, who believed like almost everyone else that she did shoot McAuley, told her their opinion, and insisted they were correct, and tried to get her to say she did not do the shooting, assuring her that statement would surely clear her. But she replied that she knew that the trigger of the gun that killed McAuley was pulled by her finger, and she could not and would not say it was not done by her. And so she went before the jury with the charge of murder against her, and admitted the killing, yet claiming it was justifiable, and she was acquitted."

****

26 November, 1887; The *Savannah Morning News*:

"If reports be true some sensational developments are likely to proceed from the Miss Elvira Ivey murder trial, which was disposed of in the Superior Court of Jefferson county last week by an acquittal of Miss Ivey. It now appears that one of the jurors in the last trial sat upon the case in a former trial, when the defendant was convicted and sentenced to five years in the penitentiary. It is reported that the juror will be prosecuted, and the matter has aroused a great deal of excitement in Jefferson county."

****

1 Dec., 1887; *Louisville News & Farmer*:

"JEFFERSON STIRRED UP.

A Complication in the Ivey Case and Much Excitement.

"LOUISVILLE, GA., Nov. 24. - [Special.] If reports be true some sensational developments are likely to proceed from the Miss Elvira Ivey murder trial, which was disposed of in the Superior Court of Jefferson county last week by an acquittal of Miss Ivey. It now appears that one of the jurors in the last trial sat upon the case in a former trial, when the defendant was convicted and sentenced to five years in the penitentiary. It is reported that the juror will be prosecuted, and the matter has aroused a great deal of excitement in Jefferson county.

"The above appeared in the Augusta *Chronicle* last Friday. It was news to the people here, and everyone looked around to discover the "great deal of excitement in Jefferson county." We have examined the minutes of the Superior Court, and find the rumor false. Wonder who sent the "special," and where did he get his information?"

****

8 December, 1887; The *Louisville News & Farmer*:

"JURORS IN THE IVEY TRIAL.

"Last week we noticed an article published in the Augusta CHRONICLE, stating that one of the jurors in the Elvira Ivey case at the second trial was also on the jury at the first trial, and we declared the report false. Since then we hear that madam rumor has settled this charge first upon Mr. J. M. Perdue and again upon his brother Mr. L. R. Perdue, both of whom were on the jury at the last trial. Neither one was on the jury at the first trial, and so the report falls to the ground. Again in some sections it has been rumored that one or both of these gentlemen heard the case tried either at the inquest, commitment, or at the first trial, and therefore were not proper jurors. This report is also false, and does injustice to both of these men who are upright, good citizens. Mr. L. R. Perdue informs us he was in Florida when the inquest, commitment, and first trial were held, and therefore could not have heard the evidence. And. Mr. J. M. Perdue tells us he never heard the case until at the last trial when he was one of the jurors."

Exhibit (8) News Sources – Murder of Solomon Jones

1February, 1921; The *Augusta Chronicle*, page 1:

"SAM G. STORY SAYS HE KILLED JONES IN SELF DEFENSE.

MUCH INTEREST IN THOMSON OVER SHOOTING – STORY'S STATEMENT, GIVEN OUT BY ATTORNEY, SAYS HE WAS ATTACKED BY DEAD MAN.

SPECIAL TO THE AUGUSTA CHRONICLE.

"THOMSON, GA., Jan. 31. – Much interest is now aroused in this section of the state over the shooting and killing of T. Sol Jones, a prominent farmer, by Sam. G. Story, a prominent planter and well-known McDuffie citizen, Sunday at noon. John T. West, one the most well-known lawyers in the state, has been engaged by Mr. Story and the following statement was made public today by Mr. West as to the direct cause of the fatal affair:

"'T. S. Jones and S. G. Story were farmers, living five or six miles southwest of Thomson, in McDuffie County. They were not adjoining neighbors, but lived several miles apart. On Sunday morning Mr. Story received a story from a negro that he was over on a farm belonging to T. S. Jones, not the place on which Mr. Jones lived, but several miles from it and somewhat between Mr. Jones and Mr. Story's, visiting a tenant on Mr. Jones' place, and that if he would come over there he thought they might be able to make a trade for him to live with Mr. Story.

"'Mr. Story accompanied by the negro who brought the message, went over to the farm and had a talk with the visiting negro. The residence of this place is several hundred yards from the public road. As Mr. Story was preparing to leave the negro's house in his automobile Mr. Jones drove up in his buggy. Mr. Jones and Mr. Story had had a disagreement of some sort several years previously about a tenant. Mr. Jones seemed angered by Mr. Story being on his premises, jumped out of his buggy and as Mr. Story's car was starting off, grabbed the steering wheel and turned it out of the road somewhat. He hit Mr. Story once with his fist and then reached down and picked up a good-sized rock and struck Mr. Story with the rock over the eye, damaging his nose considerably, and the bone above his eye and under his eye is inflamed. This practically rendered Mr. Story helpless. The car was still moving and the negro, who was in the car with Mr. Story, turned the steering wheel so as to put the car back into the road and went on down the road, holding the steering wheel for Mr. Story for some distance until he recovered sufficiently to take charge of the car and was able to run it on home. Mr. Story then got his brother, Claude, to get in the car with him and started back toward Thomson, where he expected to get surgical treatment for his wounds. This necessitated him going by the private road, which led from the public road and the negro house, which he had previously visited on Mr. Jones' place. Just before he got to this road, Mr. Jones drove into the public road with his horse and buggy, which compelled Mr. Story to stop his car. Mr. Jones then made a remark about finishing. Mr. Jones got out of his buggy pulled his knife and started toward him. Mr. Story jumped out of the car, (his brother had been driving the car, he sitting in front with him), as Mr. Jones came upon him. Mr. Jones cut at him several times, cutting his clothing in five or six different places and the knife penetrating in one or two instances to the skin, scarifying the skin but not being sufficiently deep to do any serious damage.

"'Mr. Story backed off and shot Mr. Jones once, which failed to stop him, and he still came toward Mr. Story with his knife open. Mr. Story was still backing when he shot Mr. Jones the second time, which proved fatal. Mr. Story says he did not know that Mr. Jones entertained any serious animosity toward him over their previous trouble and was much surprised when Mr. Jones attacked him without notice or further provocation. He says that he was compelled to stop his car when he was coming into Thomson, because Mr. Jones drove right across the road and he shot absolutely to defend himself. He feels if he had not shot Mr. Jones he would have been killed, and while the regrets the necessity very much, he does not see any other thing that he could have done to save his life."

****

4 February, 1921; The *McDuffie Progress*:

"MR. T. SOL JONES SHOT TO DEATH.

"Sunday morning about 11 o'clock Mr. Sam G. Story and Mr. T. Sol Jones engaged in an altercation when the latter was shot to death by the former. The shooting took place on a farm of Mr. Jones about six miles south of Thomson, between the home places of the two gentlemen, who lived about four miles apart.

"Mr. Story gave himself up and was placed in McDuffie county jail. Mr. Claud Story, brother of Mr. Sam Story, who was with him at the time of the shooting, was arrested Wednesday as an accessory to the fact and placed in jail. Owing to the prominence of both parties connected with the unfortunate tragedy, intense interest has been manifested throughout the community.

MR. T. SOL JONES.

"Mr. T. Sol Jones, a well known citizen of McDuffie county, and an active farmer, was shot and killed Sunday morning at 11:30 o'clock by Mr. S. G. Story. The sad news, swept through the county Sunday afternoon that he was dead, seemed almost to cause a momentary cessation of activity. Mr. Jones was born in McDuffie county in 1856. He had spent most of his life in this county, and was one of the best known and most loved citizens in this community. He was a regular attendant at Sweetwater church. No man was truer to his duties, truer to his friends or truer to his country than Mr. Jones. For more than a year he was in bad health, while his loved ones were sparing no pains to give him relief. But he bore it so patiently and bravely that others were greatly impressed with his strong character. His home was not only his home, but was almost everybody else's as well. His hospitality was unbounded, for he and his good wife had the happy art of making every guest feel an individual welcome. His life was uniform, consistent, reliable. True, faithful and a worthy husband. His life in the community and in the home was such that it carried always a good influence with it. While sober, discreet and careful in his speech and spirit, he had about him a vein of humor, which made him always companionable, and drew many to him of the different walks of life. He will be sadly missed in his home and in the community. His place will not be so easily filled.

"His remains were laid to rest in Sweetwater cemetery Monday at 3:30. He was a man of exceptional personal charm, and the throngs of sorrowing people from every walk of life who came to pay tribute at his funeral gave testimony of the high esteem and affection in which he was held. Rev. D. A. Howard officiated.

"The pallbearers were Messrs. J. T. Neal, Sr., W. W. Hardaway, J. E. Wilson, W. E. Hobbs, C. F. Hunt, Charlie Smith. Mr. Jones is survived by his wife and niece, Katie Maud Jones, three sisters, four brothers: Mrs. Nancy Jones, Mrs. Charity Hinton, Mrs. Fannie Arrington; Messrs. Sim Jones, S. R. Jones, Jim Jones, Pat Jones.   F. S."

****

11 March, 1921; The *McDuffie Progress*:

"CASES DISPOSED OF IN SUPERIOR COURT. - …State vs. S. G. Story, Murder. Verdict, guilty manslaughter, Sentence not less than 14 years and not over 16."

****

30 June, 1921; The *Augusta Chronicle*:

"WILL SAM STORY GET NEW TRIAL? COUNSEL PETITIONS HAMMOND. Prominent Thomsonian, Convicted of Murder, Asks New Trial. Judge Withholds His Decision.

"Judge Henry C. Hammond in superior court yesterday took under advisement application for a new trial of Sam Story, of Thomson, convicted and sentenced for the murder of Sol Jones. Attorneys appeared before the court, and the judge took the papers. He would give to reporters yesterday no intimation of the decision he would make.

"Story was tired before Judge Hammond in the McDuffie superior court for killing Jones, was found guilty and sentenced to a term of years. Both men are prominent in Thomson and are members of the best families in McDuffie county. The shooting followed an altercation."

****

1 July, 1921; The *McDuffie Progress*:

"NO DECISION YET IN SAM STORY CASE. The case of Mr. Sam Story I his appeal for a new trial was heard by Judge Hammond Wednesday, but up to Friday morning lawyers representing the case say no decision had been reached, the Judge having deferred his decision for a more careful analysis of the contentions presented."

****

9 September, 1921; The *McDuffie Progress*:

"MR. SAM G. STORY DENIED NEW TRIAL.

"Judge Hammond on Monday gave out his decision in the appeal of Mr. Sam G. Story's lawyers for a new trial for their client. The new trial was denied. It will be remembered that Mr. Story was sentenced for not more than sixteen years for the killing of Mr. T. Sol Jones last January. Mr. Story has been in jail here since the March term of court awaiting the decision of the Judge as to a new trial. It is understood the appeal for a new trial will now go to the court of appeals."

****

20 January, 1922; The *McDuffie Progress*:

"COURT OF APPEALS AFFIRMS JUDGEMENT. A decision was rendered by the Court of Appeals this week in the case of Mr. Sam Story, in which he was seeking a new trial for the killing of Mr. Sol Jones Sunday, January 30th, 1921. The higher court sustained the ruling of the Superior Court, thus denying him a new trial. It could not be learned whether any further effort would be made to change the ruling of the lower court."

Gallery

John Marion Ivey

(1853-1932)

(Brother of Elvira Ivey, Courtesy of Family Members)

Frances Sophronia Ann "Fannie" Huff Ivey, wife of John Marion Ivey (1852-1934)

(Courtesy of Family Members)

House of John Marion Ivey, built in 1910 and still standing.

(This is *not* the house where the murder occurred. Left to right: John Hillman Ivey, Annie Lou Ivey, John Marion Ivey, Fannie Ivey, Arthur Francis Ivey, Bruce Rivers Ivey.)

(Courtesy of Family Members.)

Close-up view of John Marion and Fannie Ivey, from previous picture.

Old Jefferson County Courthouse

(Photo on display at Dogwood Café – Louisville, Georgia; from the collection of Tommie Wasden. This is the courthouse in which the trial of Elvira Ivey was held. It would appear to be the old jail in the right of the photo, which is still standing.
This old courthouse was torn down and replaced with current structure.)

Old Jefferson County Jail

(Still standing, downtown Louisville, Ga.;
this is the jail where Elvira Ivey was housed.)

Door to Old Jefferson County Jail

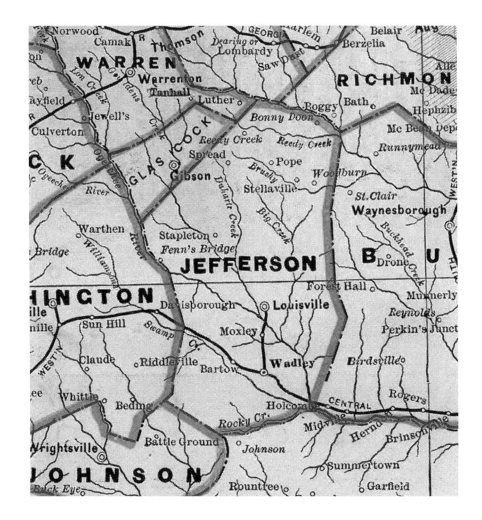

1885 Map of Jefferson and surrounding Counties.

(Notice "panhandle" area of Warren County, labeled "Luther" on this map. The murder of Jack McCauley occurred near Reedy Creek.)

> **FIRE THIS MORNING.**
>
> This morning at four the town was alarmed by the fire bell. The old Central hotel was in full blaze when discovered, and nothing could be done to save it. The building in which the News & Farmer office is and the dwelling occupied by Mr. R. L. Farmer smoked badly, and for some time it was feared they would be consumed. Both caught on top, but were quickly put out. The hotel was insured for $1000. The fire started in the room occupied by Mr. E. H. Rhodes, and everything was burned. He had gone to Atlanta. Origin of fire unknown. A lot of furniture, table-ware, &c., owned by Prof. J. E. Wright, was burned.

Clipping from *Louisville News & Farmer*, Dec. 14, 1899,

Concerning Central Hotel destroyed by fire.

This was the hotel where the jury in the first trial of Elvira Ivey stayed, downtown Louisville. The location of the Central Hotel was 101 W. 7th Street, and that site is the current "Willie House."

Photo of Willie Family Home in 2017, prior to restoration. This home was built in 1904 on the site of the old Central Hotel, which burned in 1899.

(Home at 101 W. 7th St., Louisville, Ga.)

(Photo: Courtesy of Fable Willie Candler.)

View of Willie House Restoration in Louisville, Ga.

This house was built on the location of the old Central Hotel.

To visit Louisville and see this house will give perspective as to where the jury stayed in the Elvira Ivey trial, relative to the Courthouse. Though the old Courthouse is no longer standing, the current Courthouse is at the same location.

(Photo: Courtesy of Fable Willie Candler.)

Thomas E. Watson

(1856 - 1922)

(Photo; Bench & Bar, Tenth Congressional District of Georgia, 1900)

James Granberry Cain

(1835-1910)

(Photo; Bench & Bar, Tenth Congressional District of Georgia 1900)

Fred Tutt Lockhart
(1850-1907)

(Photo; Bench & Bar, Tenth Congressional District of Georgia 1900)

J. C. C. Black
(1842 - 1930)

(Photo; Bench & Bar, Tenth Congressional District of Georgia 1900)

Roger Lawson Gamble, Jr.
(1851-1912)

(Photo; Bench & Bar, Tenth Congressional District of Georgia 1900)

J. H. Polhill

(1842-1927)

(Photo; Bench & Bar, Tenth Congressional District of Georgia 1900)

James Kollock "J. K." Hines (center)

Photo of John D. Cunningham, James K. Hines, and Tom Watson;

Taken in the Georgia State Capitol building at the Populist Convention of 1896.

(Courtesy of the Watson-Brown Foundation; Housed in the Wilson Library, University of North Carolina at Chapel Hill, Thomas E. Watson Papers, Southern Historical Collection.)

Judge J. K. Hines
(1852-1932)

(Close-up of Previous photo)

Judge Samuel Lumpkin

(1848-1902)

(Courtesy, the Georgia Capitol Museum)

Hickory Hill, Home of Tom Watson, McDuffie County, Ga., purchased 1900

(Courtesy, Watson-Brown Foundation)

Photo of home of Tom Watson

As it appeared in 1880s, Thomson, Ga.

(Courtesy, Watson-Brown Foundation)

Headstone of Col. W. D. Tutt
(1838-1906)

Pine Grove Methodist Church, Lincoln County, Georgia

Headstone of Fred Tutt Lockhart

(1850-1907)

Summerville Cemetery, Augusta, Georgia

Headstone of Alex B. McCauley
(1875 - 1897)

Smyrna Methodist Church, Wilkes County, Georgia.

Smyrna Methodist Church,

Wilkes County, Georgia

Headstone of Mrs. Francis E. McCauley (1840-1916)

Smyrna Methodist Church, Wilkes County, Georgia

Col. Rev. James Stapleton

(1824-1888)

Tombstone of Elvira Ivey Barron (1863-1939)

Zeta Cemetery, Tennille, Ga. – Washington County.

Tombstone of James R. Barron

(1858-1921)

Zeta Cemetery, Tennille, Ga. – Washington County

Entry in Record of Warren County Superior Court, 9 Oct., 1885;

"The State Vs. Sol. Jones – Seduction; Solomon Jones formally arraigned and pleads not guilty, Wm M Howard, Sol Gen"

"State Vs. Sol Jones: Indictment for Seduction, Plea in Abatement: It being admitted by the State Counsel that the act alleged in the plea in abatement in the above stated case is true it is ordered that the plea be overruled.

Samuel Lumpkin, Judge."

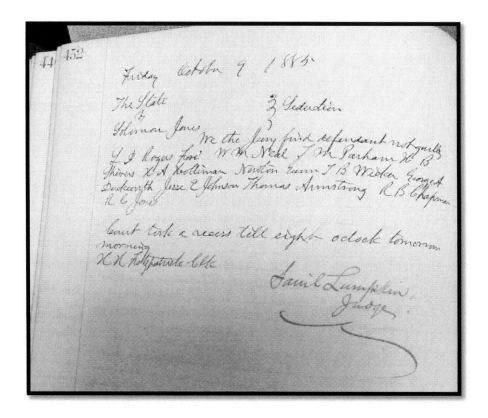

Entry in Record of Warren County Superior Court, Friday 9 Oct., 1885:

"The State Vs. Solomon Jones – Seduction: We the jury find defendant not guilty; L. D. Rogers, Fore', W M Neal, T B Parham, N B Shivers, H A Holliman, Newton Gunn, T B Widon, George A Duckworth, Jesse E Johnson, Thomas Armstrong, R B Chapman, R E Jones… W N Fitzpatrick Clk., Samil Lumpkin, Judge."

Death Certificate of Thomas Solomon "Sol" Jones

McDuffie County, Georgia; January 30, 1921; showing cause of death to be "pistol shot – homicide."

Bruce Ivey Road, in northern section of Jefferson County, off Hwy. 296.

(Named for Bruce Ivey, son of John Marion Ivey; Bruce was the nephew of Elvira Ivey. The house belonging to John Marion Ivey, where Jack McCauley was murdered, was just off this road. The land is currently owned by a kaolin company, and the house is no longer standing.)

Little Briar Creek Baptist Church
Warrenton, Georgia

Reedy Creek Baptist Church
Stapleton, Georgia

(Old photograph; this is how the Church would have appeared in the 1880s)

Reedy Creek Baptist Church

(The church as it currently appears. The original log church built in 1817 was destroyed by fire; later the church was rebuilt, and this structure is part of the current building, with modifications and additions.)

Sweetwater Baptist Church
Thomson, Georgia

(Photo: Courtesy Kelsey Dees)

Unfortunately, I was unable to find a picture of Miss Elvira Ivey… suffice it to say, she was most beautiful.

Made in the USA
Columbia, SC
14 April 2022